WITHDRAWN

WILD AUSTRALIA

WILD AUSTRALIA

by

Michael K. Morcombe
A.R.P.S., A.F.I.A.P.

TAPLINGER

First published in the United States in 1972 by
TAPLINGER PUBLISHING CO., INC.
New York, New York

Copyright © 1966 by Michael Morcombe
All rights reserved.
Printed and bound in Hong Kong

No part of this publication may be reproduced or transmitted
in any form or by any means, electronic or mechanical,
including photocopy, recording, or any information storage
and retrieval system now known or to be invented, except by
a reviewer who wishes to quote brief passages in connection
with a review written for inclusion in a magazine, newspaper
or broadcast.

Published simultaneously in the Dominion of Canada by
Burns & MacEachern Ltd., Ontario

Library of Congress Catalog Card Number: 70-179495

ISBN 0-8008-8322-5

Acknowledgements

THE AUTHOR wishes to thank the following contributors, whose photographs provided a wider coverage of animal life: the National Travel Association for Poplar Gum and Kookaburra; Gary Lewis for Koalas, Leadbeater's Possum, Feather-tail Glider, Ringtail Possum, Emu, Dingoes, Frilled Lizard, Grey Kangaroos, Platypus and Red Kangaroos; S. and K. Breeden for Flying Fox and Water Skink; Eric Lindgreen for Red-tailed Phascogale, Honey Possum and Numbat; Patricia Slater for Fat-tailed Dunnart; Gordon De 'Lisle for Red Kangaroo; Irene Morcombe for Everlastings, Red Leschenaultia, Isopogon, Pink Boronia, Clematis and Cowslip Orchid; Graham Pizzey for Lyrebird (colour); L. H. Smith for Lyrebird; R. Garstone for Black Swan.

CONTENTS

Chapter		
	THE EUCALYPTS	7
	WRENS	15
	BANKSIAS	23
	HONEYEATERS	31
	CREATURES OF THE NIGHT	37
	PARROTS COCKATOOS LORIKEETS	47
	THE ARID LANDS	53
	BIRDS BENEATH THE GROUND	65
	MISTLETOES	71
	FOREST LIFE	75
	THE WESTERN WILDFLOWERS	91
	DEPENDENT ON WATER	104

Introduction

AUSTRALIA IS FAMED for its fauna: for the strange animals that have been symbolic of the southern continent since the first recorded description of a kangaroo by the navigator Pelsart on the western coast in 1629.

Kangaroo, Koala, Platypus or Lyrebird have been the basis of almost every Australian wildlife book, though many others among Australia's creatures are not only more colourful, but in way of life and in adaptation tell an equally fascinating story of evolution in an isolated continent.

Some, like the diminutive Rufous-crowned Emu-wren, are unlikely to be seen by the casual observer. Others including robins, wrens and possums may be familiar visitors to farm and suburban garden, but for the visitor from another land, less familiar than the kangaroo.

In this book kangaroo, koala and others commonly accepted as constituting the wildlife wonders of Australia are given second place after birds and animals of greater beauty, and of more than equal distinction for a fascinating way of life.

It is not surprising to find within a continent stretching from the tropics to the Antarctic Ocean, and including desert, rainforest, mountain and sandplain, a vast number and wide variety of native plants and birds, so that a single volume such as this can contain no more than a sample, no more than a hint, of the wealth of wild Australia.

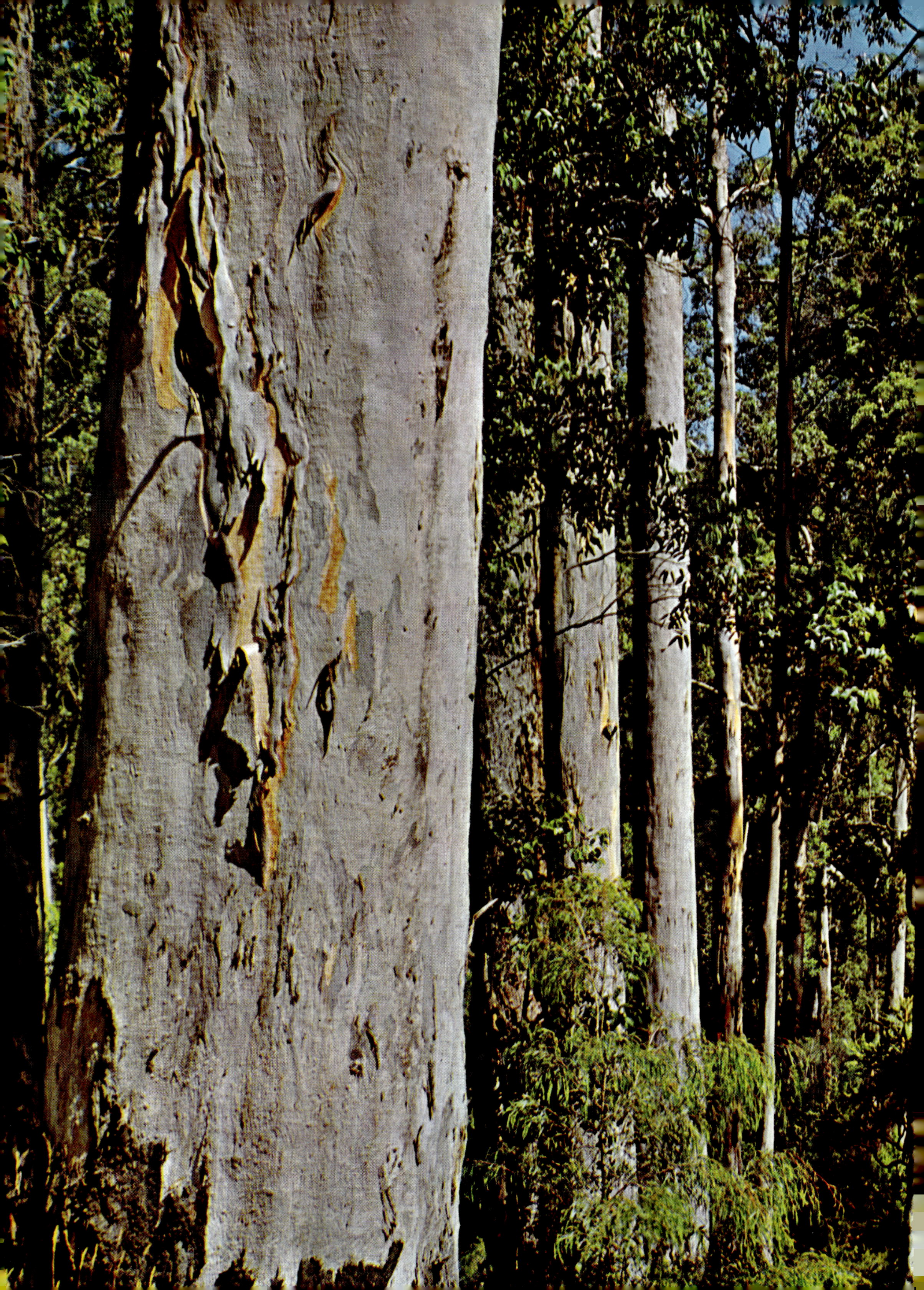

THE EUCALYPTS

A FOREST MAY be said to resemble a city, constructed and populated with trees and birds, shrubs, and mammals, reptiles, insects, fungi and the vital microscopic bacteria.

Among the trees there is competition for light and for crown space above; for root space and for water and minerals in the soil. Of the millions of seeds germinating, few struggle up to a place among the giants. Every plant and wild creature of the forest must have its place: a niche, or space in the food chain, which it can hold against strong competition by showing some specific superiority.

A single tree may directly or indirectly supply a variety of birds, plus a host of other creatures, and each creature will concentrate on the part of the tree it is best adapted to exploit in its search for food. No one tree could long support the multitude of its dependents, but the segregation of feeding habits of which it is an example extends through the forests, and through other biomes — as the terrestrial life zones are known — from tropical rain forest to schlerophyll forest and to mallee or mulga scrub.

Flowers might attract lorikeets and honeyeaters. On the leaves tiny insects are taken by pardalotes and thornbills. Soft seed capsules bring parrots, but hardened woody gum nuts may require a more specialized bird, like the Red-capped Parrot which

Forest gums usually have small flowers, but in massed profusion these may hide the foliage and cover a tree. Most are creamy-white, like these of the Marri, Eucalyptus calophylla. *Others may be pink or red, but the greatest single flowers of eucalypts are those of the stunted inland mallee forms.*

The twisted trunk of a **River Red Gum,** Eucalyptus camaldulensis, *may be attractively streaked and mottled with shades of brown, yellow, grey and white. These trees line the bank of rivers through inland Australia from east to west.*

is able to extract the seeds without cutting through the capsule — a difficult if not imposible task.

Seeds falling from dry gum nuts would be found by a ground-feeding rosella or one of the small *Neophemas*, perhaps one like the Elegant Grass Parrot. Beneath the bark shelter spiders and insects, prey of those specialists of tree trunk and branch, the sittellas and treecreepers. Upper branches may nourish a parasitic mistletoe, whose sweet and sticky berries are principally the food of the scarlet-and-black Mistletoe Bird.

Around the roots, in soil made fertile by the decaying leaves, worms, caterpillars and the like, are hunted by robins which cling sideways to the treetrunk, motionless but for the occasional characteristic flick of wings. They drop to the ground at intervals to take some near-invisible morsel. Which of the robins, would depend on the locality: Scarlet, Flame, Rose-breasted, Red-capped, Yellow, Hooded, and White-breasted are among the many members of the group.

Green plants are the basis of every food chain. Upon these plants feed the herbivorous insects, birds and animals. These in turn are food for predatory animals — or plants in the case of sundews and pitcher plants. Death brings scavengers, from bird and animal carrion feeders to the fungi and bacteria which finally reduce the life materials to the simplest elements, plant foods to be taken up for a further cycle.

Dense coastal forests show greatest evidence of the struggle between plants. There the seedlings fight upwards through dense undergrowth towards the light; epiphytes, parasites and saprophytes steal food or a place in the sun; and climbing vines may strangle and kill great trees in their own upward race. A Queensland jungle fig which germinates on the branches and drops strong roots to the ground may kill its supporting host and be left standing on a hollow 'trunk' of latticed roots after the dead support has rotted and fallen. From the start it is assured a place in the light.

Ochre trunk and branches name the **Salmon Gum.** *On richer parts of inland plains these trees raise tall umbrellas of dark, glossy leaves high above surrounding scrub.*

Soaring trunk and branches of a Lemon-scented Gum stand clean and fresh against deep-toned summer skies. The gums are a race of trees apart; unexcelled in variety and adaptability, and with few equals for size or beauty, they dominate the bushland of a continent, and in exceptional diversity number more than six hundred species and varieties. Their leaves may be broad stem-clasping ovals or long, pendant crescents; glossy green or glaucous, powdered blue; or wine-red and golden on new spring and summer shoots.

Most eucalypts have hanging leaves, twisted so that the direct power of mid-day sun is not full on a flat surface but glancing across one side or the other. To take advantage of this the leaves of gums are structured with photosynthetic cells on both surfaces.

Eucalyptus orbifolia, *the Round-leaf Mallee, named for its orb-shaped leaves, is an inland mallee of slender stemmed and straggling habit. Like many others of the interior it has branches and leaves dusted with silver-white powder. Mallee form of growth is frequently adopted where harsh conditions prevail. Numerous short, slender stems develop from a durable underground root stock which is protected from heat and fire.*

Eucalyptus forrestiana, *Fuschia Gum — a shrubby little tree of dry western inland plains. Pendulous buds and fruits give colour long before and after the yellow filaments show.*

OPPOSITE:

The Mottlecah of the West Australian sandplain has leaves whitened by the powdery bloom adopted by some desert plants as a protection against drying winds. The flowers are the largest in the genus, being three inches or more across. Flower colour of the Mottlecah, E macrocarpa, *varies from deep crimson and rose pink to orange-yellow and creamy-white.*

This mallee dwarf, Eucalyptus tetraptera, *has great square buds, and bright seed capsules which hang on the tree long after the pink flower stamens have dried and fallen.*

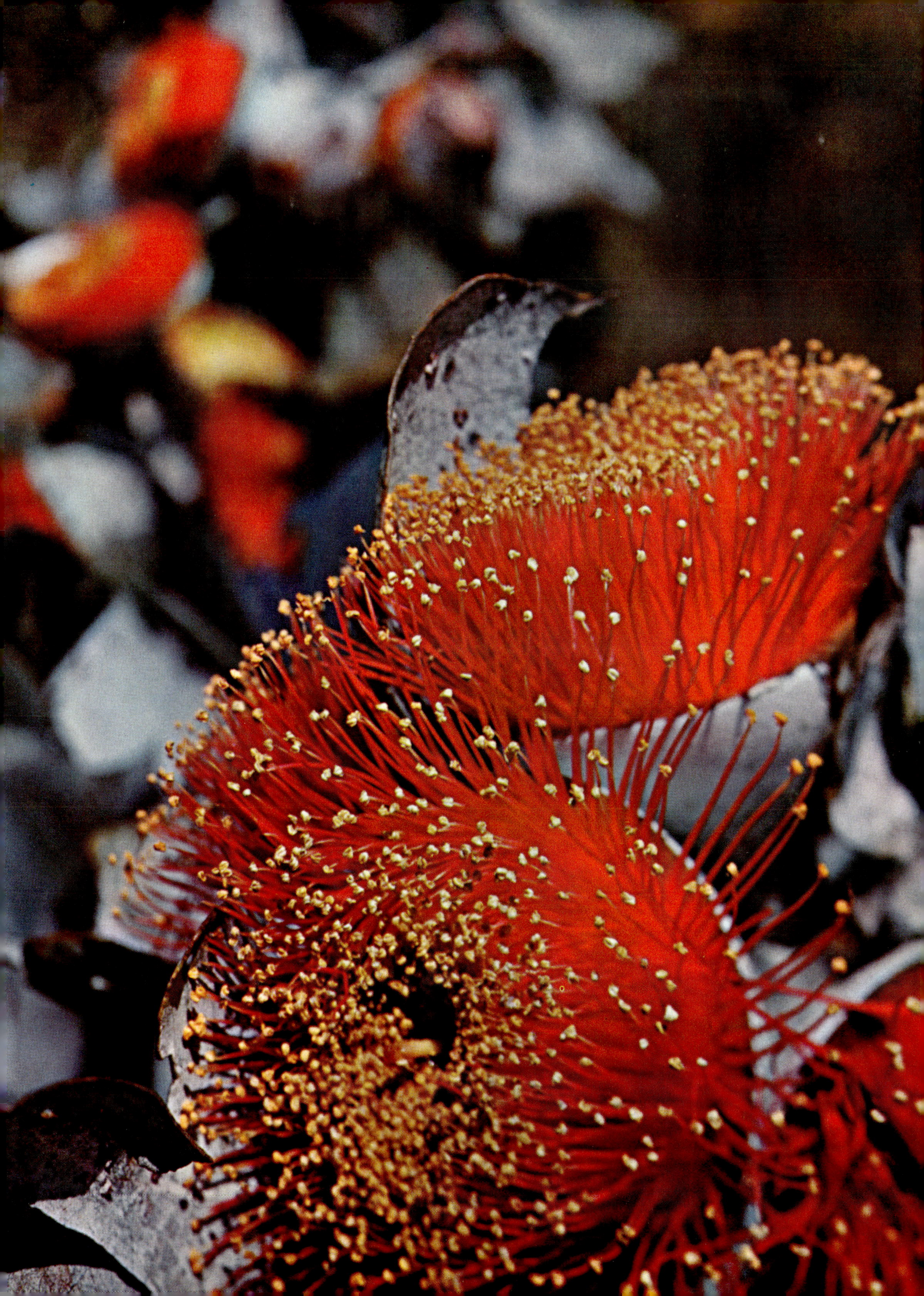

Not so obviously competitive is the life struggle of trees of the open, or of the scrub formations of sandplains. There the fight is not for space and light, but for services of bird and insect pollinators, for the dispersal of seeds where they are most likely to germinate and for survival of seedlings which must get down their deep taproots to permanent supplies of underground water before the next long period of drought.

There is competition among trees and shrubs for soil moisture, so that the spacing between plants becomes greater as conditions become more arid towards Australia's dry centre. These inland and sandplain gums, though but small and stunted mallees and shrubs in many instances, bear great flowers, far larger than those carried by forest trees. Most forest eucalypts have small, creamy-white flowers, made conspicuous only by their appearance in massed bunches. Some spectacular exceptions include the tropical "Ngainggar" or Scarlet Gum, *E. phoenicea*, from the Gulf of Carpentaria; the widely-cultivated Red-flowering Gum native to a very restricted area of the south coast of Western Australia, and a red-flowered form of the White Ironbark of South Australia.

Flowers of eucalypts are preceded by buds which with developing flower parts covered and protected by an operculum, may hang on the tree for half a year before the cap is dropped and stamens unfold. Often the calyx tube from which the flower unfolds is brightly coloured and with sculptured shape, as seen in *Eucalyptus tetraptera*, the Square-fruited Mallee, and *Eucalyptus Forrestiana*, Forrest's Marlock. With these forms the calyx is red and glossy, with buds and fruits hanging all over the shrub for months before and after flowering, and appearing as their most attractive feature, for the red or yellow filaments are relatively inconspicuous.

With others the operculum may be ridged or indented, rounded, conical or with a long central spike. This operculum is made of petals fused together as one structure, forming the cap over developing stamens. In fact the name '*Eucalyptus*' means 'well covered', and refers to this little cap. As the flower expands the operculum cracks around, and falls, leaving a flower without petals, but with a radiating mass of coloured filaments, each capped with a golden, pollen-dusted anther.

Sometimes the bud caps contrast in colour: *Eucalyptus erythrocorys* a small, white-barked western tree when flowering may at first glance appear to be carrying both red and white flowers, for each operculum is bright red, the filaments rich yellow, and calyx tubes contrast in deep emerald green.

Flower colour in the *Myrtaceae*, the Myrtle family to which eucalypts belong, is limited to the range of warm colours and whites — from crimson, scarlet, pink, orange, and yellow to creamy white or greenish white.

Gums of Australian forests rank among the world's highest, topping three hundred feet. Smooth, sheer trunks rise a hundred feet or more to the first branch. Bark varies from the dark rough texture of blackbutts to the smoother, creamy white of the Lemon-scented Gum; the rich salmon pinks and tans of the Salmon Gum, and the pink-and-salmon-and-grey shades on the great cylindrical trunks of the karris. The bark may be patterned by cracks into squarish pieces marked by oozing red gum, lined by the zig-zag tunnels of insect larvae on the Scribbly Gum, or mottled by flaking sheets of old white and grey bark peeling to show pale yellow or fawn tints across the solid trunks of the River Red Gum.

So characteristic is bark formation that it has become the basis of some keys to identification; very necessary where there are more than six hundred species and varieties of eucalyptus trees. Gums will readily hybridize, particularly when disturbed by clearing and regrowth, or when planted outside the natural regions. Even the introduction of the larger, wider-ranging hive bees, which may carry pollen over wider areas than the native bees, is thought to have increased hydridization amongst gums.

Eucalypts predominate in Australia's bushland, and extend in the stunted but often most beautiful forms far inland, as well adapted to extremes of heat and dessication as to ice and snow on peaks of the Australian Alps. Under the harsh conditions of extreme dryness many gums assume a "mallee" form. From a large knotted root rise numerous slender stems which may not reach to more than ten or fifteen feet. Fire, always a feature of the dry scrub, may destroy stems and branches, yet in this bulbous rootstock is always the potential of rapid regrowth. Many which grow normally as mallees may develop as trees with a single, larger trunk when planted in more favoured regions.

The smooth-barked Poplar Gum, Eucalyptus bigalerita.

Eucalypts are classified as members of the *Myrtaceae*, one of the largest plant families in the Australian continent, with more than three thousand species, and including not only gums, but also plants of *Melaleuca, Beaufortia, Calothamnus, Kunzea,* and *Callistemon* — which are a few of the most decorative groups. Also within the Myrtle family is a group characterized by seeds which germinate on the soil among loose leaf litter and debris. The single seed is retained in the withered flower, which is of light and fluffy form, and when dropped from the bush is not easily buried. The most conspicuous examples of this form are to be found among the feather flowers of the *Verticordia*, in which the calyx lobes are finely divided to form a soft, feather-like structure. *Verticordia nitens*, a tall western plant, bears its feathery flowers in mushroom crown massed above the foliage, which is completely hidden by their dense layer. Flowering in summer, and standing close-packed on three-foot stems, it covers the sandy flats with gold brighter than any field of ripened wheat, stretching over acres at a time beneath scattered banksia trees.

In every way the eucalypt and its family forms a remarkable group, not only containing the world's tallest hardwoods, and forests of great commercial value, but also a host of Australia's most decorative wildflowers, ranging from the massed spectacle of the flowering gum to the delicately detailed structure in the feather flowers.

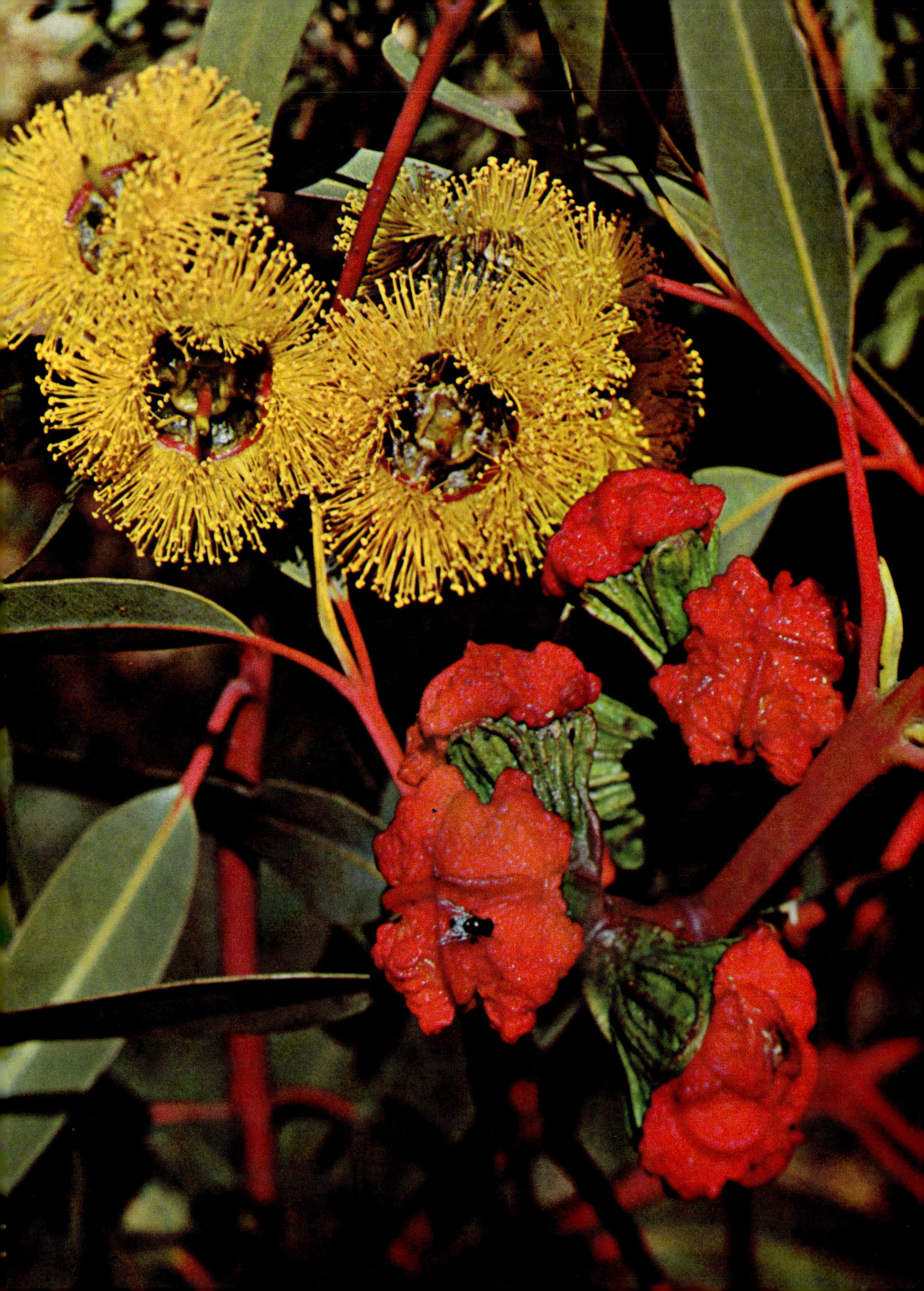

WRENS

FOUND ONLY IN Australia is a group of colourful birds known variously as Blue Wrens or Fairy Wrens. "Wren" includes the blue wrens of the genus *Malurus*; the insect-sized, long tailed Emu-wrens—genus *Stipiturus*—plus other less colourful individuals including scrub-wrens and grass-wrens.

All are characterized by long tails carried jauntily upright. While of great interest for their exquisite colouration and dainty form, the wrens of the genus *Malurus* (the blue wrens) have also attracted considerable attention by their social organization; groups of birds holding territories instead of individual pairs as with most birds.

For many years certain wren species have been noted for the apparent excess of females, even in the nesting season. For this the wrens have occasionally been dubbed "Mormon Wrens". Recent observations have shown however, that while it is more common for the bright male to be accompanied by two or three grey-brown wrens, not infrequently there may be two or even three of these colourful males, together with one, two or three of those grey-brown birds assumed to be either females or young males not yet in breeding plumage.

OPPOSITE:

This small gum from the central western coast shows flowers first in scarlet, then as bud caps fall, in the bright yellow of unfolded stamens. Each Ilyarrie tree appears splashed in red and yellow. Botanically Eucalyptus erythrocorys, *the white-trunked little tree flowers in late summer months.*

Clad entirely in rich, iridescent blue and glossy black, the Banded, or Splendid Wren, was well named Malurus splendens. *The wren's high-pitched, reeling song is a characteristic sound of the bush where the bird may be glimpsed through the scrub as a tiny flash of blue.*

Studies of banded and numbered wren populations have indicated that in each group is an established breeding pair comprising the dominant male and a breeding female. Often this pair alone may hold a territory, but usually the group is more complex, and more than one male in colourful plumage may be present. In such larger groups these males include the dominant or breeding bird and one or more younger "supernumary" males, which may have a varying richness of plumage colouration, frequently equalling the dominant male in brightness. Such supernumary, non-breeding males, together with the several non-breeding females often present, play a role important to the group and to the success of the species as a whole. Although the supernumary birds are often old enough to breed they remain for a time in the family group and earn their way by feeding the young of the breeding pair, which is then able to raise second and even third broods in quick succession.

Though males within a group rarely conflict, all will react by attacking, physically or by song battle, any intruder of the same species which happens to enter the well-defined family territory. Nest construction and incubation of the eggs apparently are tasks for the nesting female of the group.

Observations show that for much of the year the younger males loose their brilliant plumage, and are scarcely distinguishable from the females until several years old, when the coloured plumage becomes permanent.

All members of the family group share the work of feeding the nestlings though some may be much more enthusiastic about it than others. One frequently encounters the nest where the colourful male or males deliver a few early morning insects, then leave this chore to the females; yet at some other nests the male may be the bold, conscientious parent, assuming a major part of the task of rearing the young. These differences appear among individuals of many species, and become particularly evident when many hours must be spent near a nest for photography.

When the young leave the nest, and have grown independent of their parents, they remain in the family group to help feed and care for the next offspring.

The wren most studied has been the Blue Wren, *Malurus cyaneus*, of south-eastern Australia. This bird was shown to be multi-brooded. That is, a pair will raise many sets of offspring while the favorable season lasts. This enables the species to be reproductively more successful within the limits of a variable climate.

The number of young fledged is for any bird, and particularly for the small passerines very often less than the number of eggs laid. The losses are due to a wide variety of causes, ranging from stormy weather or the activities of a cuckoo whose egg may cause the wren to abandon her whole clutch; to the attacks of predators including snakes, kookaburras, cats and marsupials.

Wrens breeding in family groups produce more young growing to independence, per adult, than would the same number of adults if all in breeding pairs, even though there may be only one pair breeding in the family group. The presence of the other 'spare' adults to care for young birds just out of the nest, permits not only a greater number of clutches of eggs to be laid, but also results in a much greater number of surviving young at the end of the season. The surplus birds of the family group eventually set up territory as members of breeding pairs, in their own or nearby territory.

Among the blue wrens of the genus *Malurus*, the presence of excess males or females at nests has been observed for a number of species, including not only the closely studied *Malurus cyaneus*, but also the Splendid or Banded Blue Wren, *Malurus splendens*, the Red-winged Wren, *M. elegans*, and the Blue-and-White Wren, *M. leuconotus*.

These wrens have also attracted attention by their well developed distraction displays. When a nest is threatened the adults give a convincing "broken wing act", or "rodent run" display, during which the performer puffs up its feathers, droops

As the female Splendid Wren turns to fly from the nest a male arrives with food for the young. The long tail which is held jauntily upright when the birds are perched or hopping across the ground foraging for insects, streams behind in flight.

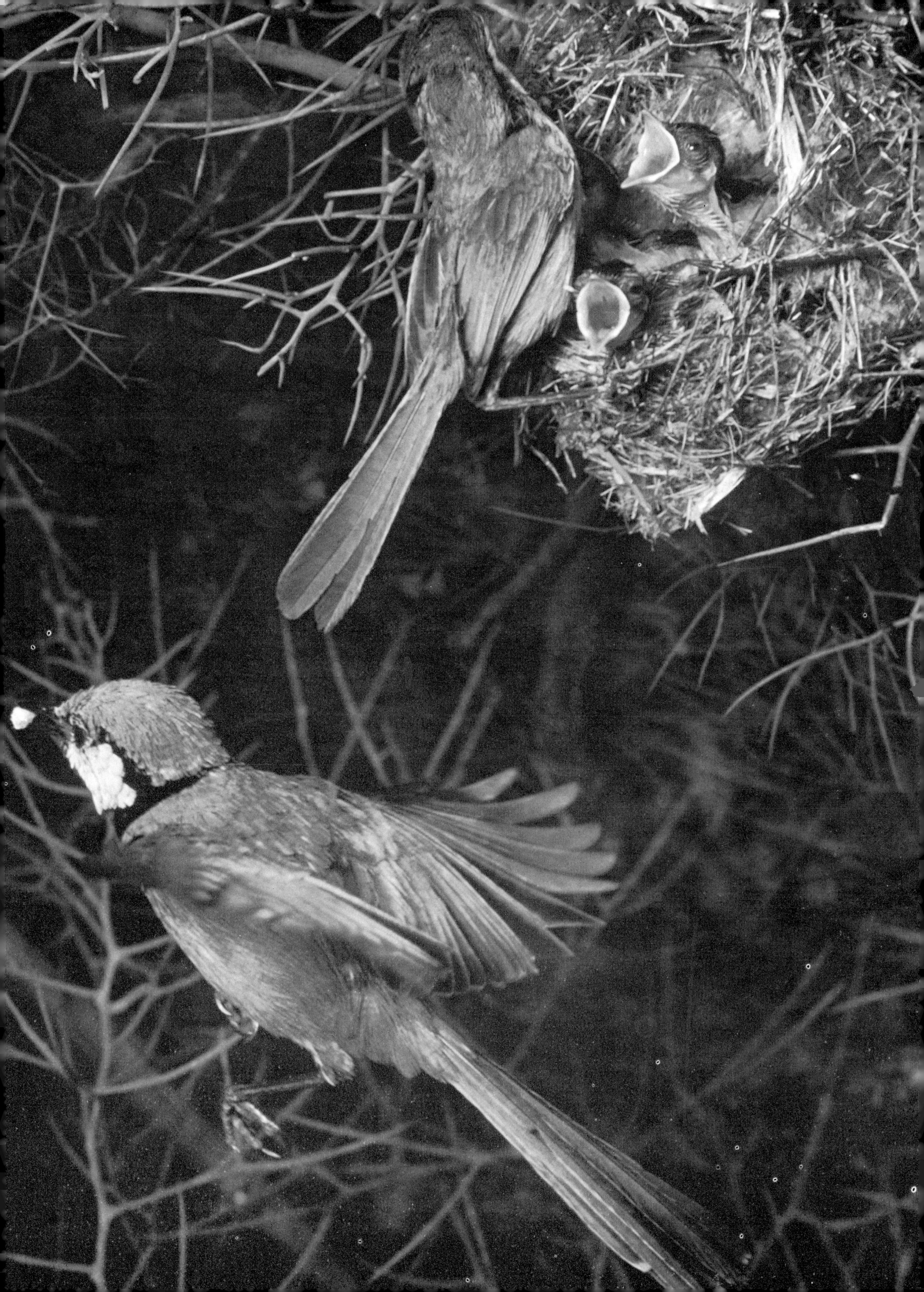

Perched at the entrance to its well-concealed nest, this brightly-plumaged male Red-winged Wren shows a variegated pattern of colours, particularly the chestnut shoulder patches for which it is named. Difficult to distinguish are other chestnut-shouldered wrens — Variegated Wren, Blue-breasted Wren, and the Lavender-flanked Wren of the Kimberlies. Fortunately, habitats of the southern species differ sufficiently to allow the casual observer to identify by locality, but real difficulty can ensure where the ranges of the desert species overlap.

This Red-winged Wren, Malurus elegans, conceals its fragile, roofed-over nest where the pendant leaves of a grass-tree tangle with the debris of the forest floor. Great care is needed to follow the shy and secretive birds to their nest. Three small, speckled eggs complete the clutch.

Flying emu-wrens resemble large insects: the great, straight-flying grasshoppers of the north, where this Rufous-crowned Emu-wren is found. These are among the smallest of Australian birds, and hidden for the most part in spinifex clumps, momentarily bouncing across the intervening patches of red earth, but not often seen. This species, Stipiturus ruficeps, with the Southern Emu-wren and the Mallee Emu-wren is named for the peculiar long tail feathers, which in pattern resemble the plumage of the emu.

The globular nest of the Rufous-crowned Emu-wren is concealed in prickly Triodia. So well does its dry grass structure blend with the yellowed stems and dead heart of a spinifex clump that it would usually be found only by meticulously tracing the bird's movements until the hidden site is shown.

OPPOSITE PAGE:

In the distance may appear to be the fluttering form of a common white butterfly — until a second glance reveals the darker colours of a flying Blue-and-white Wren. The flickering white wings of this bird are a conspicuous feature as it flies low between small bushes of the scrubby flats of samphire and saltbush. Here both male and female carry food towards a nearby nest. Behind the flying male is the red soil and, distant, the spinifex flats of its natural environment.

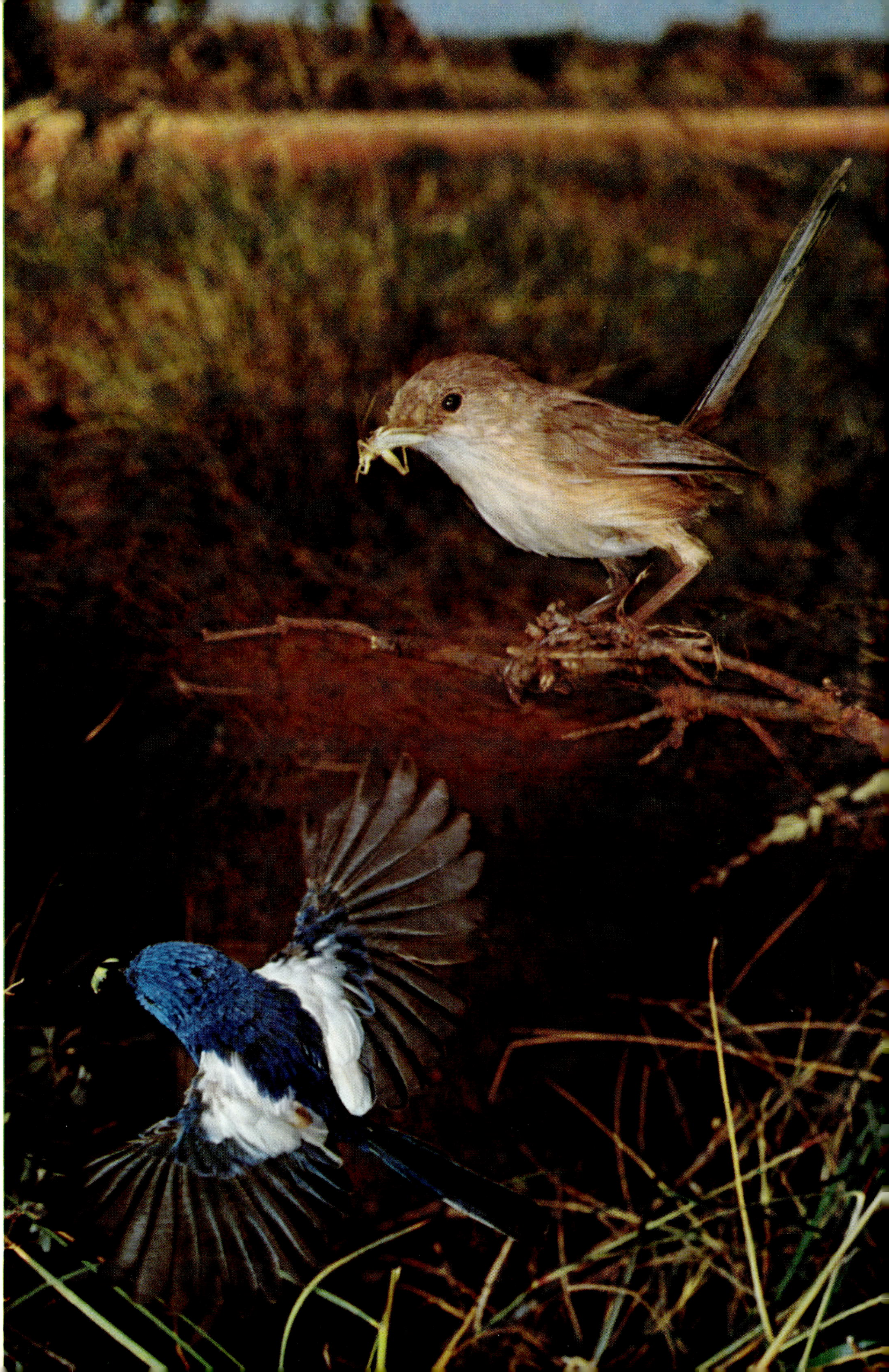

The nests of the wrens are usually well concealed in thick, often thorny scrub or tangled vegetation near the ground. All construct a roofed nest with a side entrance; building and incubation are tasks for the female. This wren is the female of the Variegated Wren. Like most females of the group she is relatively colourless, with only the long tail showing blue. She differs from the females of other species in the prominent eye markings. The male of the species Malurus assimilis *appears in the following colour plate.*

the tail (normally carried so jauntily erect), and scuttles along the ground in a swaying, wavering run away from the nest. Pursued too closely, it will fly, but return to repeat the trick until the predator is led from the nest area.

Another remarkable mechanism to protect a hidden nest was recently reported. The female brooding in the nest fell like a stone to the ground, and actually hit with a slight but audible thump — then scurried along the ground and into the bushes. Was this bird imitating a naturally falling object — a gum nut, perhaps? To fly directly from a nest would immediately reveal its location.

The hiding place for the hooded nest varies from species to species. The Banded Blue Wren usually selects prickly wattle scrub, and constructs a strong nest of grass two or three feet above the ground, where it is often not well hidden. The Red-winged Wren, a shy inhabitant of the densest undergrowth along creeks of the Darling Ranges and through the karri forest, builds a more fragile nest of the usual domed, wren pattern. The most favoured situation for this nest of grass, leaves and bark shreds is beneath a short grass tree, or blackboy, where masses of dead, narrow leaves lie on the debris of the forest floor. Such a situation defies discovery of the nest except by painstakingly following the path taken by the wrens as they hop through the dense undergrowth. Even when the concealing blackboy is finally found, a careful search through the hanging leaves and debris is usually necessary to reveal the hidden nest.

The Variegated Wrens' nest is also well hidden (photo) but its habitat are the scrub clad coastal sand-plains. Blue and White Wrens show a preference for the lowest scrub or samphire flats across the continent.

But of all wren nests, the award for concealment must surely go to that of the Rufous-crowned Emu-wren, *Stipiturus ruficeps*, an inhabitant of the spinifex plains from the arid north-west to the heart of the continent, and whose southern limits of distribution are delineated approximately by the Tropic of Capricorn.

The elfin emu-wrens are unique chiefly because of the reduced number and peculiar structure of their six tail feathers — much longer than their tiny bodies which are barely two inches long. Their total length is stated as being less than five inches. Because the pattern of these feathers resembles that of Emu feathers, the three species of the genus *Stipiturus* are known as Emu-wrens. The two other species of this genus, the Mallee Emu-wren and the Southern Emu-wren are found in the inland south-east and southern costal regions respectively.

Constructed of dry grass and tucked into a thick clump of prickly spinifex, the nest of the northern Rufous-crowned Emu-wren ranks among the masterpieces of nest camouflage. Not that it is deeply hidden in this dense *triodia* — it is in fact perched towards the top — but its colour and outline blend almost invisibly with the general appearance of the dead interior of the yellow-green spinifex tussock.

Whether hidden in the spinifex clumps, or bouncing across the bare red earth of these arid regions, the tiny Rufous-crowned Emu Wrens rarely show themselves. Only if their tiny, high pitched calls are heard can their presence be detected and, causing many a fruitless search, there is in those regions an insect responsible for an exasperatingly-similar squeak. When flying from bush to bush these wrens, with long-plumed tails streaming behind, look for all the world like large insects — like the great, straight flying grasshoppers of the north, which resemble the wrens both in size and in tawny colour.

Many other wren species fill a wide variety of habitats covering the entire Australian continent, from the tropical north with its Purple-crowned

Two male elegans *assist in the feeding of young in the nest. Both are members of one family group: one would be the dominant male — the breeding bird and chief defender of the nest territory. Within the group may be one or two mature but subordinate males, but more commonly several of the greyish female or immature birds.*

As the male Red-winged Wren waits perched on a fallen Bull Banksia seed cone, the female flies from the nest. These wrens are the largest of the genus, but shy inhabitants of the densest undergrowth along south-western forest creeks and swamps.

and Red-backed Wrens, through the central deserts (the Turquoise Wren, the Black-backed Wren, the Variegated Wren and the Blue-and-white Wren), to the south — Splendid, Red-winged, Blue-breasted and Southern Emu Wrens. The insular Black-and-white Wren is found only on western coastal islands.

Everywhere the jaunty little birds are favourites. The flash of blue brings admiration from all. Yet how few are well known, except where their distributions happen to border on the cities of men.

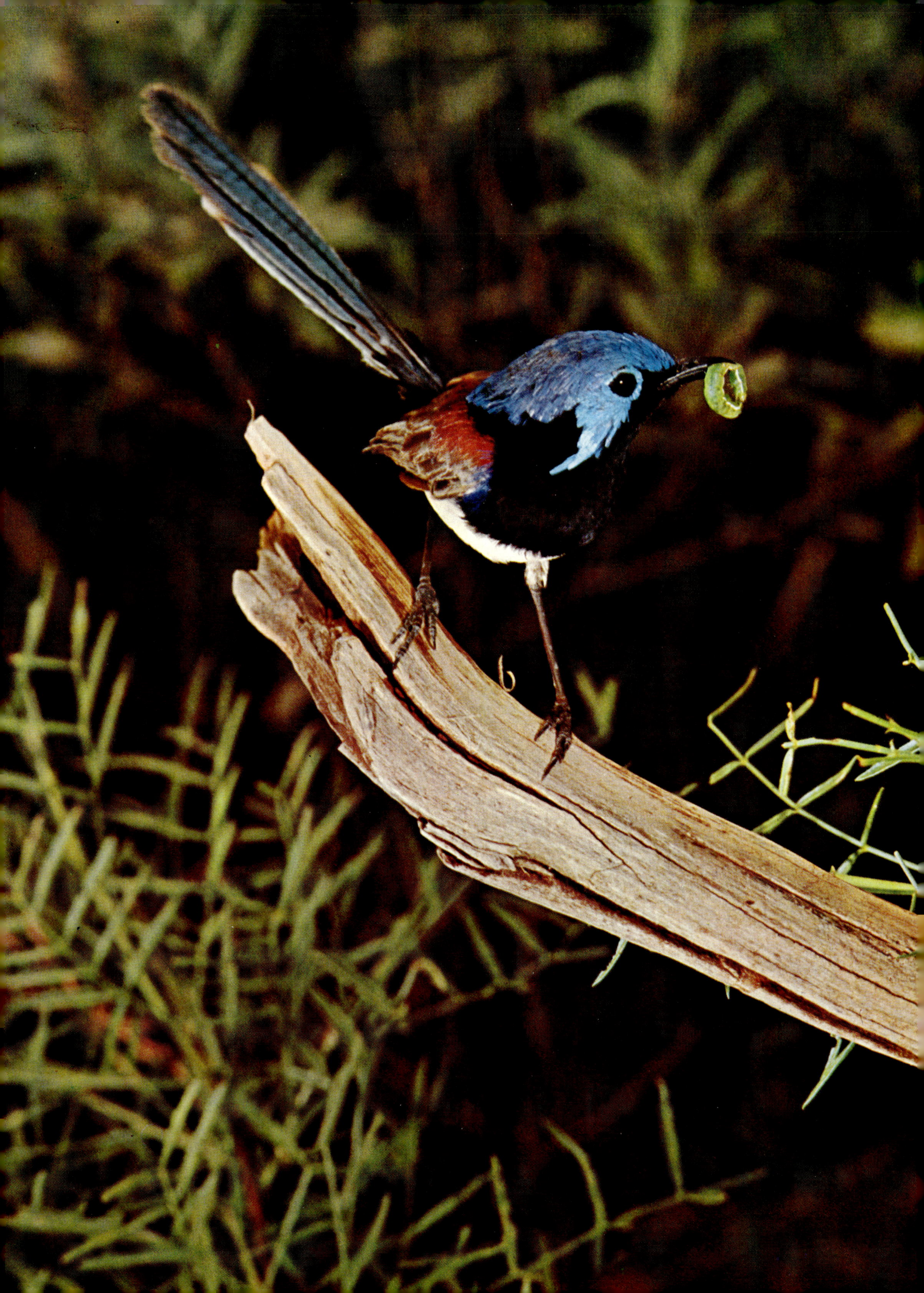

BANKSIAS

WITH FLOWERS often so large that each may be seen at a distance of a hundred yards or more, yet with every one retaining intricate floral detail and patterned structure inviting closer study, the many banksia trees and shrubs are an outstanding and unique part of the Australian flora.

Most of the banksias are distinguished by the exceptional size of their flowers and the finely structured spikes or cones. Actually each spike (which in some species, like the yellow Bull Banksia, *B. grandis*, may reach a foot and a half in length) is not a single flower, but a complex of close-packed, spirally-arranged flowers. Arrayed around the perpendicular spike these massed flowers form a great, colourful, conical or cylindrical structure, generally called 'the flower' though it may contain thousands. In some species, as *B. spherocarpa*, the Round-fruited Banksia, the inflorescence is more globular in shape.

Banksias are generally in hues, shades or tints of red or of yellow. They range from crimson, scarlet, pink, orange, deep and pale yellow, to some unusual bronze effects, and to white, and green-tinted whites and yellows. None are blue;

LEFT:

The Variegated Wren. The male of this species may be distinguished from that of the similar Red-winged Wren by the black rather than blue breast. This is more an inland and arid-country bird, which reaches the sea only where dry country extends to the coast in north-western Australia.

The State of Western Australia has a disproportionate share of the magnificent Banksia *trees and shrubs, which in that state grow principally on the sandplains — home of many spectacular wildflowers — and on coastal patches of sand soil.* Banksia coccinea, *the Albany or Scarlet Banksia, from the southern coast, is one of forty species found only in the west.*

one bears huge oval spikes turning light-grey, soft and woolly, which remain for months on the shrub, looking for all the world like sleeping koalas.

As the thousands of tiny flowers arrayed around each spike burst open, its colours and finely detailed patterns change. Each flower is contained in a slender tube which opens to release the long style and golden-tipped anthers. Flowers at the base of the cone may open first: a band of new colour or new pattern of floral detail spreading from the base, to cover the whole flower spike.

Perhaps the most striking example of this changing colour is the golden-flowered *Banksia*

prionotes from sandplains near the western coast. A distant tree, perhaps twenty or thirty feet high, may appear to be carrying both white and golden cones. A closer look shows that any individual cone, a composite spike nine or ten inches long, may be entirely smooth and satin-white, or may show an expanding zone of bright orange comprising thousands of the tiny opened flowers, each bursting from a fluffy white cover to show its colour. This intense cadmium band creeps up over the surface to envelop the entire structure, and each silvered cone is transformed into a golden-orange cylinder. When massed against dark blue-green foliage, or thrust aloft in typical prominence against the sky, these intermingled great white and golden cones of the Orange Banksia create a truly spectacular effect.

Even more arresting is another tree of these sandplains — *Banksia ashbyii*, which bears longer floral cylinders, each attaining a length of nearly a foot, and with a deeper and more intense colour than the preceding species.

In this form, no significant colour change occurs as the packed flowers of each long spike open. All stand out in the same rich hue. Found well to the north, where grey skies are rare, this tree holds high these great sunlit cones in striking colour contrast against the deep blue above.

For intricate detail more reminiscent of the finest work of a jeweller or sculptor of miniatures in metal than of a living flower, the crimson *Banksia occidentalis* must be among the best of its family. Its wealth is not displayed in spectacular show, for in nature these trees grow clumped in dense masses, in swampy situations, with the large flowers half-hidden in foliage. A close view is needed to reveal the flowers' intricate detail: the fine, wire-like structures of burnished crimson arrayed in rhythmic order up each large spike; the slender vivid green of the newly-formed spikes, each meticulously inscribed with clear diagonal lines marking out the developing flowers.

Also of the south coast of the western corner of the continent is another red banksia: the Scarlet, or Albany Banksia, *B. coccinea*. Its short wide cones are marked out in vertical bands of red and white, and prominently displayed on the tips of slender stems.

Small, damp sandy flats and valleys between the harder forested ridges may shelter clumps of scarlet banksias. At times, perhaps as regrowth after fire, a patch of an acre or two in extent may be so densely covered in slender young banksias that one must force a way through. Every one of the thousands appears as a slender little stem with few branches, clad in rounded, clasping leaves and capped with a terminal cone of scarlet. Scattered throughout are the older trees, reaching fifteen or twenty feet high. Unfortunately such patches of massed *coccinea* are but sparingly scattered through a restricted south-coast habitat in the west — all too easily wiped away before the ever-advancing cash crops.

The Swamp Banksia, *B. littoralis*, which bears long greenish spikes opening to golden yellow, shares with a pink-flowered species, *B. menziesii*, a sandy coastal-plains habitat: indeed most banksias are inhabitants of sandy country, few thrive if planted in heavy soil or clay. One exception is the Bull Banksia, *B. grandis*. This is a small tree reaching to twenty or thirty feet, bearing huge cylindrical spikes which change from green to yellow as the profusion of flowers mature and burst out. This is a tree of the laterite and the heavier soil, and forms a lower storey beneath the red-gum and jarrah. In the southern parts of its range, as near the jagged Porongorup peaks, the tall bright floral cylinders of this banksia may attain a length of eighteen inches, each rising from a whorl of foot-long leaves which are deeply serrated, zig-zag fashion, to the midrib.

Often quite as attractive as the flowers is the new growth. Banksias tend to grow in short spurts, rushing upwards a foot or two at a time through spring and summer months. Their flower spikes are always borne erect at the ends of branches, blocking further growth. Bottlebrushes — species of *Callistemon*, *Kunzea*, *Calothamnus*, and *Melaleuca* — continue the stem growth through the axis of the flower, but in *Banksia* each flower cone marks the end of a straight branch. As the banksia flower forms, shoots develop in the stem just below, to burst out in sudden fast growth, by-passing the terminal spike, and surrounding the woody seed follicles which follow.

Soft, frond-like new growths thrust upwards past the flower spikes. Covered with a russet tomentum which can be highly ornamental, these new shoots and their radiating leaves may cap the tree with warm colour even when no flowers show. The effect is prominent in *B. grandis*, where the great zig-zag leaves first show in rust and cinnamon

A developing spike of Banksia media, *a south-coastal shrub, shows the intricate detail in arrayed flowers which expand and unfold, changing the size and colour and texture of the great floral cone: in some species, particularly the white and golden* Banksia prionotes, *dramatic colour changes occur.*

OPPOSITE:

Nine inch flowers in white and orange standing high above the foliage and clearly visible at a distance, as in the background here, make the Orange Banksia, B. prionotes, *a commanding tree of the sandplains, where most other growth is small. Flowers develop from green spikes to silky white, then burst out in bright colour which finally covers the cone. Flowering extends through summer months, when the banksia has for company other golden wildflowers: the Christmas Tree — the parasitic* Nuytsia, *and acres of golden feather flowers,* Verticordia nitens.

Long cylinders of Banksia Ashbyii *scarcely show change in their intense hue as component flowers unfold, but take on a richer tone and rougher texture. Displayed high against strong blue northern skies they create bold colour contrasts which make this tree perhaps the most spectacular of all banksias.*

Each serrated pink cone ridged with white transforms slowly into a rough-textured orange cylinder as the thousands of individual flowers open in a band spreading up from the base. This banksia of sandy coastal plains bears six-inch spikes for many months, and is a favoured nectar source for the honeyeaters, including particularly Red Wattle-birds, New Holland, Spinebill, and Brown Honeyeaters. At night it may occasionally yield nectar to a probing honey or pygmy possum.

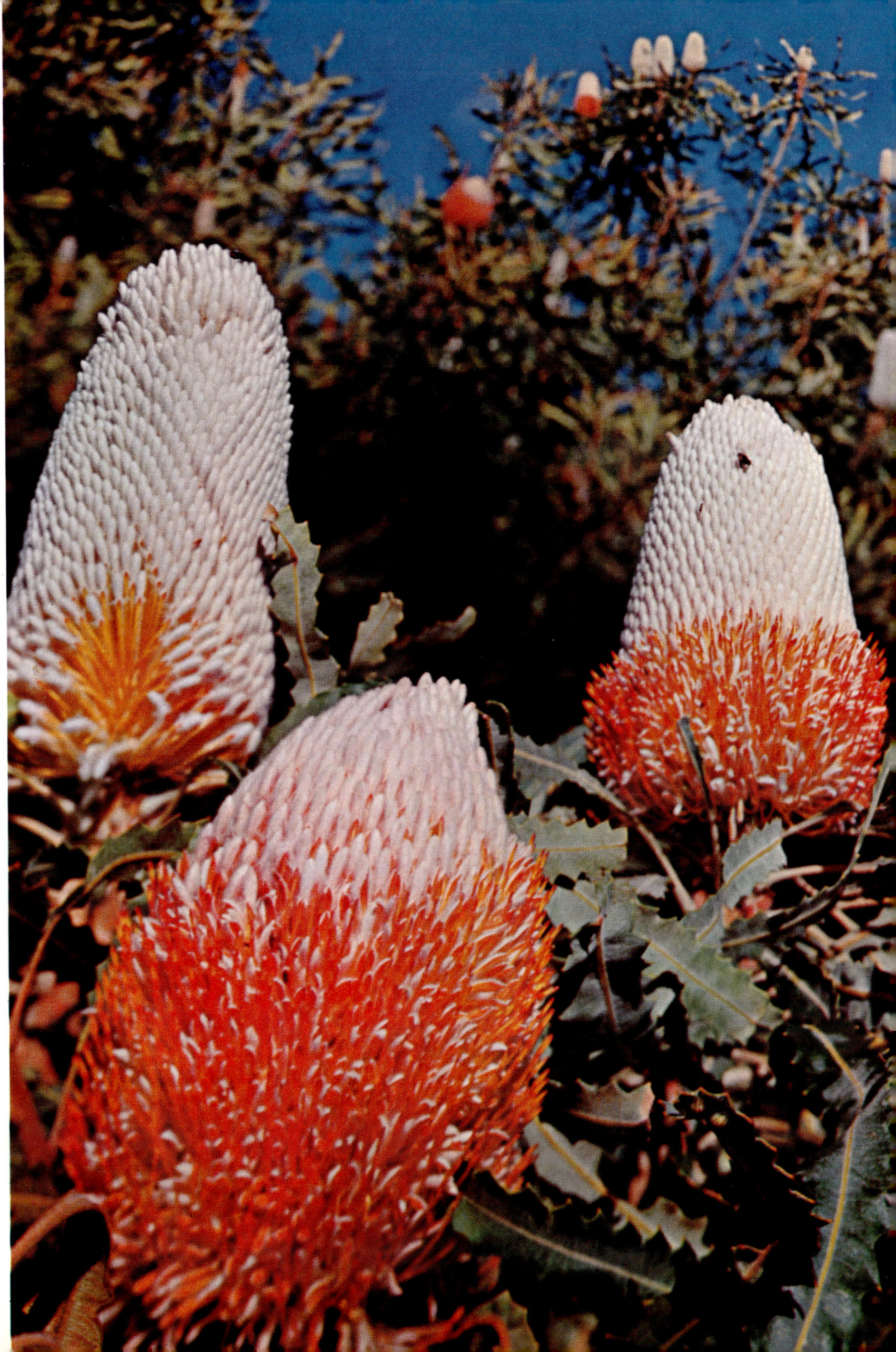

tones, and in *B. Baxteri* (back cover) which has similar but smaller leaves.

Each upward spurt stops as suddenly as it began: the soft leaves and stem thicken and harden and shed the ornamental rust and ochre-tinted surfaces. Later, new buds will begin to swell beneath flowers and at the ends of branches, marking the beginning of the next upward rush.

Though banksias are found in most States, forty of the fifty-one species are confined to Western Australia. Most are trees or shrubs, which may occasionally be dwarfed by conditions of exposed coastal headlands or desert areas — but confined to the south-west are four species which grow completely prostrate, never assuming shrub or tree habit. These creeping banksias have developed from the more usual erect forms. Stems which once were vertical now lie along the ground beneath surface sand and litter; leaves which once radiated from the stem still emerge from its lower surface in the ground, but creep around and upwards so that all appear to have sprouted from the top side of the prostrate stem. Again, leaves radiating from a vertical stem are extended horizontally, with glossy green surface uppermost. Those rising from the creeping stem in the ground are borne erect, but have still retained differentiated dull and glossy surfaces though each side now has equal sunlight presentation. Eucalypts also have leaves which hang vertically, and the internal structure has adapted to take advantage of the sun on both sides. Instead of having a single layer of photosynthetic palisade cells beneath the upper surface like most deciduous trees, the gums have two such palisade layers, and are equally smooth and green on both sides.

The erect leaves of the prostrate banksias have not yet modified in this way. The photosynthetic palisade is limited to one side. Only on the semi-arid sandplains is there any tendency, through the development of an all-over grey woolliness, for the leaf surfaces to become uniform. It is clear that the prostrate banksias have evolved from erect forms. Their nearest relationship to other banksias appears to be with forms found high in the Stirling Ranges, where the prostrate forms may first have developed long ago.

For sheer size of flower, banksias offer great potential in cultivation as feature trees of unusual distinction and great beauty: few others can match them with flowers of equal prominence or perfection of detail.

The species combined as the genus *Banksia* lend their name to a whole family of genera, grouped together as the Banksia Family, or *Proteaceae*. Widespread in the southern hemisphere and richly developed in Australia, where seven hundred species occur, the *Proteaceae* includes among its Australian genera *Grevillea, Isopogon, Conospermum, Hakea, Dryandra,* and others.

Grevilleas, with long racemes of flowers of characteristic banksia shape, range through from the colours of fire — scarlet and crimson, and the intense orange of the Flame Grevillea, *G. excelsior* — to the creamy-white of the huge inflorescences of *Grevillea aestivalvis*.

Isopogons include the various cone bushes and drumsticks, with large terminal flower heads. *Isopogon latifolius* of the Stirling Range peaks is the largest flowered of these; *Isopogon dubius* is another attractive pink-flowered form of rose cone bush, but is found on wet clay forest-flats.

Various *Conospermum* shrubs are "smoke-bushes", named for delicate grey-white plumes held above the foliage.

Hakea includes many tall shrubs with bright red, pink, purple or white flowers, of bottlebrush or of globular sea-urchin shape. Its species range from coastal forests to the deserts where the Corkwood, *Hakea lorea*, with large, creamy-white flowers, may be the only sizeable tree on the barren spinifex plains.

Restricted entirely to south-western Australia is the genus *Dryandra*, with forty-eight species of yellow, golden and bronze-flowered shrubs.

While no other group within the *Proteaceae* can quite equal the splendour of the genus *Banksia*, combined they help make the banksia family one of the richest of the Australian flora.

The River Banksia, B. verticillata, is a forest tree, growing on swampy creek margins: soil and moisture conditions very different from those of most of its relatives of open plains and sandy soils.

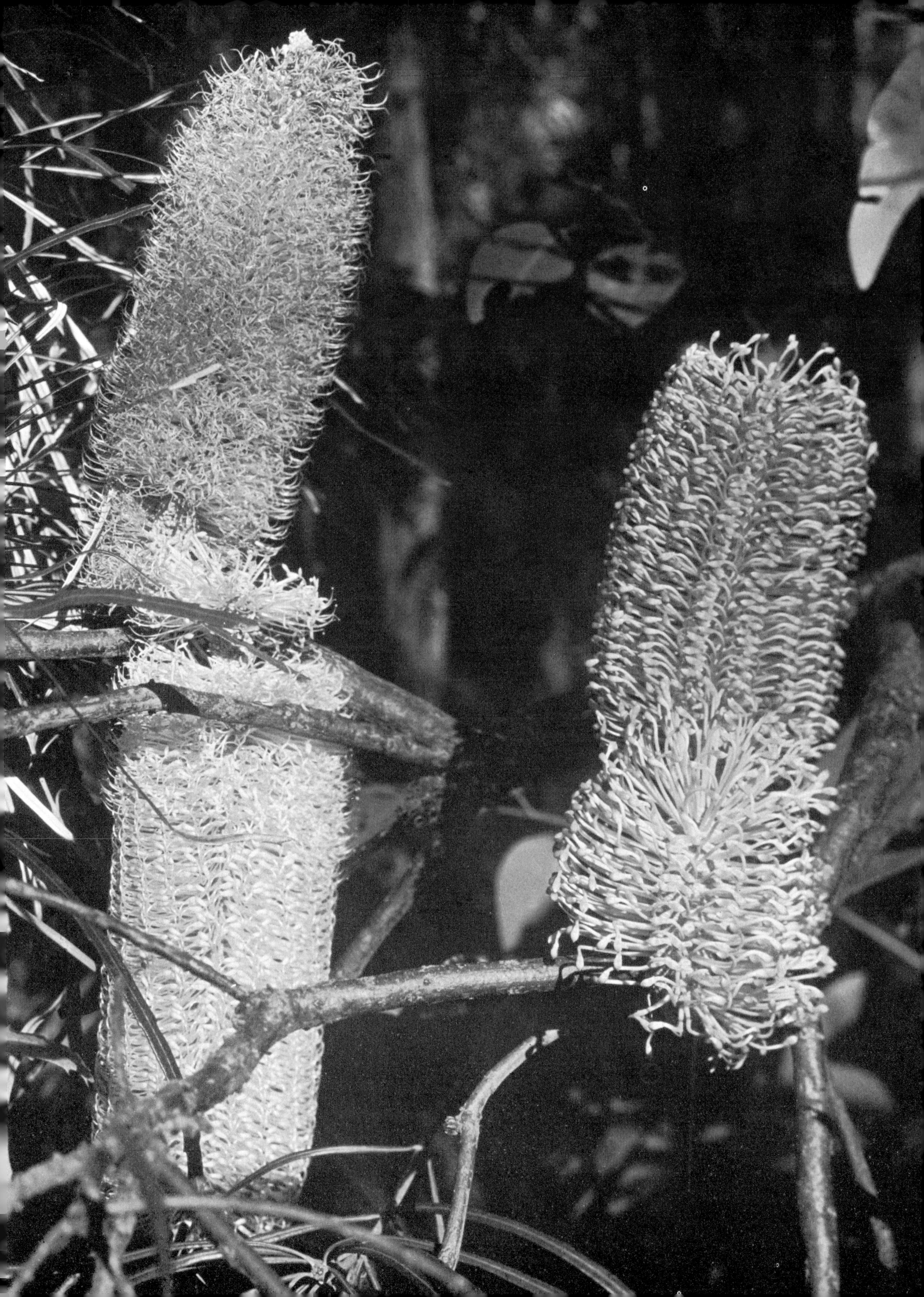

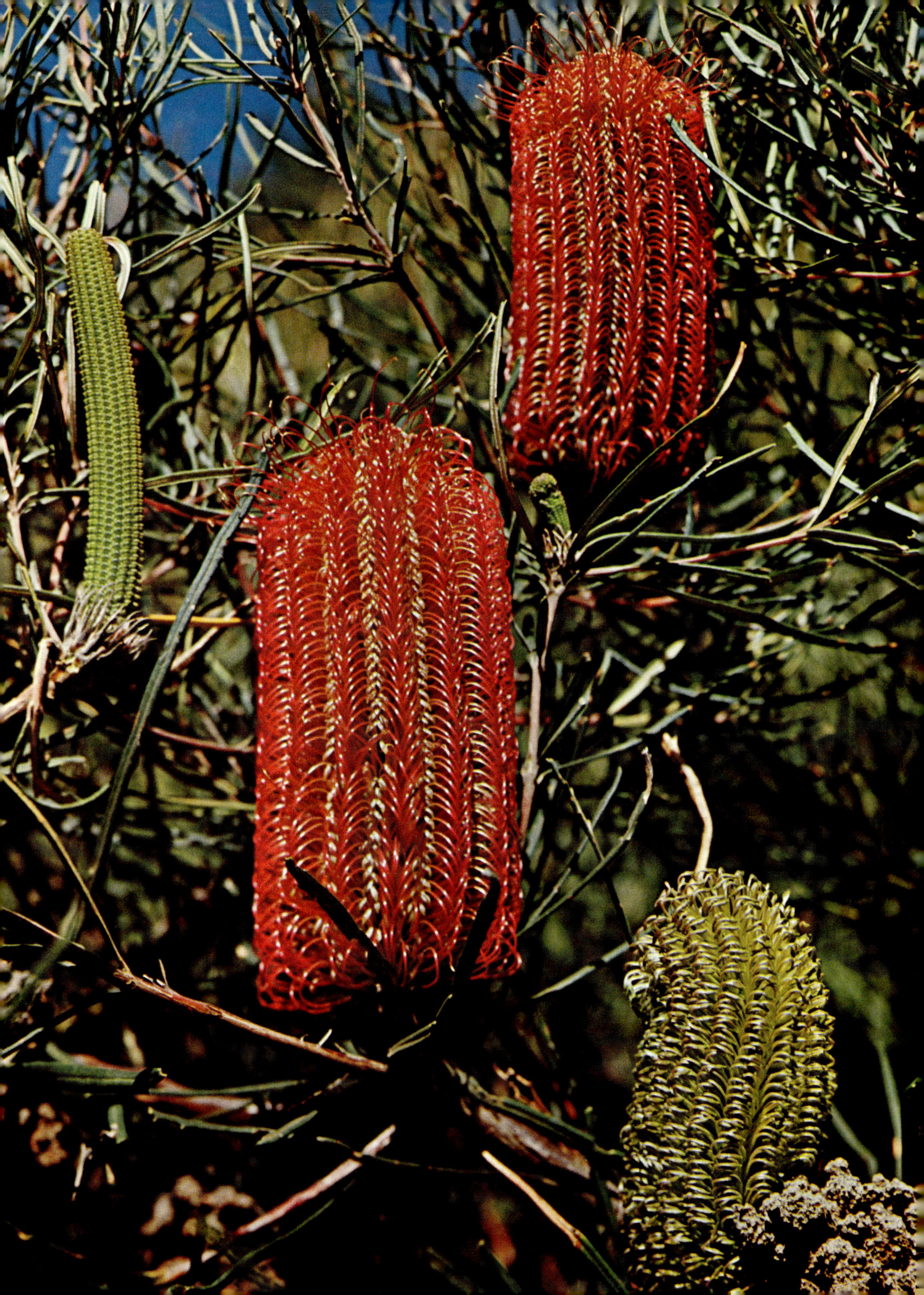

HONEYEATERS

Throughout the year in Australian bushland and forests, the wealth of flowering trees and shrubs sustains a host of nectar-feeding insects, birds and small marsupials.

Eucalypts, banksias, grevilleas and hakeas abound; each a family of species differing in structure, in flowering season and in distribution, so that in every month of the year there are wildflowers showing.

There are in *Eucalyptus* alone some six hundred species and varieties; in the banksia family seven hundred Australian forms. Though the greatest profusion of blossom is reached in spring and summer months, flowering continues throughout the year with no real winter chill to freeze the nectar flow. It is hardly surprising that there should have developed such creatures as honeyeaters, dependent upon the bush flowers.

As each plant species bursts into flower at its favoured time, some in scorching summer sun, others beneath grey but mild winter skies, honeyeaters of more than a hundred species across the continent probe the flowers for nectar. With constant brushing of plumage against bunched stamens, or by the thrusting of beak and head among the flowers these honeyeaters are believed

OPPOSITE:

Banksia occidentalis *is a crimson swamp banksia from the cool, moist south coast. Half-hidden in tangled foliage, each burnished cylinder is a masterpiece of finely ordered structure, expading from a slender green spike on which the lines of developing flowers are sharply inscribed.*

Feet outstretched, and wings beginning a final forward beat, a New Holland Honeyeater, Meliornis novae-hollandiae, *lands on a dryandra where nectar and insects are ample lure for birds which must perform the service of transferring pollen from flower to flower on feet and beak and plumage.*

to assist in a major way the pollination of wildflowers and forest trees, and to have been instrumental in the evolution of flower structures, particularly the bizarre kangaroo paws, the Sturt Desert Pea, and many of the *Myrtaceae*, including the eucalypts.

Honeyeaters, *Melaphagidae*, are small nectar-feeding birds of the south-west Pacific region, forming a typically Australian group distinguished by adaptations for the nectar diet. With an extensile tongue, brush-tipped and laterally curved to form a long tube, the honeyeaters are equipped to probe between the stiff, wirelike flower structures of banksia or dryandra, to penetrate the long tubes of kangaroo-paw and grevillea, and to part the narrow opening to the nectary of the Sturt Desert Pea. For most honeyeaters, insects form an important part of the diet, these being captured at flowers or in the air. Some differences are evident between species — when feeding young in the nest the Western Spinebill gives insects almost exclusively, but much of the food given by the yellow-winged New Holland Honeyeater seems to be nectar.

Few honeyeaters are truly migratory. Most are nomadic, wandering from region to region within restricted areas, the extent of which depends upon the requirements of the bird, the geographic location of the region, and upon its variety of flowering plants — all factors which may determine whether the honeyeaters will be compelled to move on periodically to new areas.

Long-flowering plants in some areas enable some honeyeaters to remain completely sedentary. Such a shrub, of great value to several honeyeaters, is the yellow-flowered Hollyleaf Dryandra, *Dryandra sessilis*, which not only provides a nectar supply for some nine months of the year, plus nest sites in dense, pungent-leaved foliage, but happens also to match exactly in colour the yellow wings of its most common honeyeater associate, the New Holland Honeyeater.

In drier inland regions — the mallee and mulga country where flowering follows the rains — honeyeaters are forced to wander further, but observations suggest that the quick return of honeyeaters after rain may be more due to the availability of water than to the nectar flow, which follows some time later. Among the eucalypts, the great flowers of the mallee forms seem well adapted to bird pollination, and of course provide nectar as the lure for the attentions of the bird. Not only the great floral structures of *Eucalyptus macrocarpa* or of *E. pyriformis*, but also the massed flowers of forest trees use birds as pollinators. The gift of nectar must surely be repaid as the birds climb among the flowers, brushing pollen from anthers to stigma with beak and with plumage. Here insects may be less useful, for the smaller ones crawl through the rigid stamens of the larger flowers, and may not touch the pollen-tipped parts of the flowers; the pollen does not readily shake off the anthers under the light touch of the insects. Larger, introduced hive bees are probably now among pollinators of eucalypts and their wider-ranging flights may have contributed to increased hybridization.

Particularly adapted to honeyeater pollination are the various kangaroo-paws, the beaufortias, the banksias, and some of the pea flowers, of which the Sturt Desert Pea and the green Bird Flower are significant examples.

In order that pollination be successfully effected it is necessary that a few grains of pollen be transferred from the stamens of one flower to the stigma of another. This requires that any avian pollinator must frequently touch or brush against the pollen-laden anthers, and subsequently touch its pollen-

New Holland Honeyeater at its nest, hidden among the pungent pointed leaves of a dryandra — a bush which not only supplies a bird with nectar and a safe nest site, but also happens to have flowers which match exactly the pure yellow wing patches of this honeyeater.

daubed plumage against the sticky stigma of another flower, whence the pollen grains will grow downwards to achieve the final phase of fertilization in the ovary, where the seeds will later form.

Kangaroo-paws are conspicuously bird flowers, for at the tip of each, looking like the claws of the paws are the yellow anthers, spread where a probing spinebill could hardly fail to brush its crown and, at the next paw, to bring this pollen-dusted spot against the curved stigma a little further in the tube. Also marking the paws as bird flowers is the absence of any insect landing platform comparable to the petals of most flowers, or the perfect little platform that is the labellum of an orchid. For most small birds a perch of perfect scale and placement exists as the curving, red-felted stem, from which the nectar tube of each paw may be reached as it opens in its turn. Perhaps best known of the kangaroo-paws is the red-and-green species, *Anigosanthos Manglesii*, shown in the colour plate with a Western Spinebill — the bird most often seen perched on its gently-swaying red stems, and reaching into the flower tubes.

Converging in evolution towards this paw-like structure, so admirably suited to bird pollination, are certain of the flowers of *Calothamnus* and *Beaufortia*. The crimson flowers of both *Calothamnus chrysantherus*, and of *Calothamnus sanguineus*, the Silky-leaved Blood-flower, have a paw-like shape, which is achieved in the former case by the arrangement of five staminal bundles and, in the latter, by the union of the two upper staminal bundles to form a wide pollen brush which generously dusts the forehead of any probing honeyeater. Smaller stamen-bundles complete the tube shape, and contribute to the dusting of the feeding bird. Within the paw-shaped tube a long stigma is curved to touch the pollen-daubed head of each honeyeater thrusting down towards the nectar source.

The flowers of banksias are spirally arranged in great cones or spikes which may reach a length of nearly a foot and a half. When a honeyeater lands, feet and beak and plumage gather pollen among the stiff array of variously-coloured flower structures, and when the bird flutters across to the next spike it takes the pollen which will achieve the flower's purpose.

Although many pea flowers are insect-pollinated, some of the most successful and widespread of the Australian forms have adapted to bird pollination.

A spinebill honeyeater uses long, downcurved beak to advantage in probing among the stiff structures of the Banksia grandis *flower spike.*

OVERLEAF:

Birds land so effortlessly that it is difficult to understand the complexity and exquisite timing of the act. At one moment the bird is in flight, twisting among branches at a speed difficult to follow. The next instant it is perched nonchalantly, wings folded, on a stem or twig still swaying from the touch of landing. The bird must come in fast enough to maintain lift, yet land accurately on a small perch which may be jerking in gusty wind. From full flying speed it must suddenly brake, wings cupped and tail fanned out at the last instant: this it can do though wings may be forced to awkward positions as the bird dives through intervening foliage.

High speed photography captures an instant of action which could be seen only as blurred motion. Western Spinebills, Acanthorhynchus superciliosus, *may be seen probing the deep tubular flowers of kangaroo-paws and grevilleas, or the wire-like structures of banksias.*

OVERLEAF OPPOSITE PAGE:

Clinging to the tall flower spike of a Swamp Banksia, B. littoralis, *a diminutive Brown Honeyeater seems ready to drive its long curved beak deep among the massed flowers. Both banksias and kangaroo-paws, together with many other Australian wildflowers are adapted to bird pollination; the honeyeaters in turn benefit by the great variety of nectar flowers, for some are out in every month of the year.*

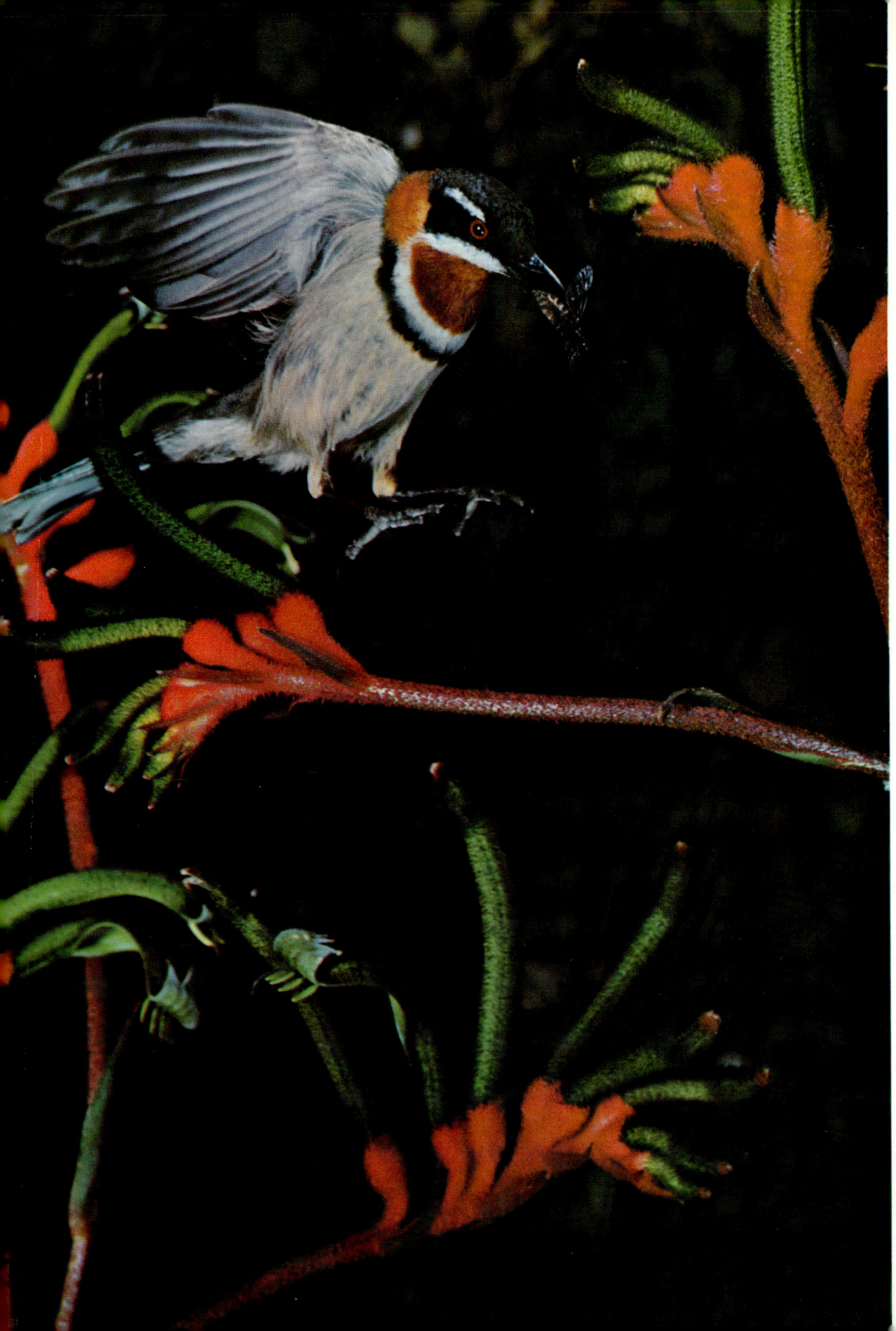

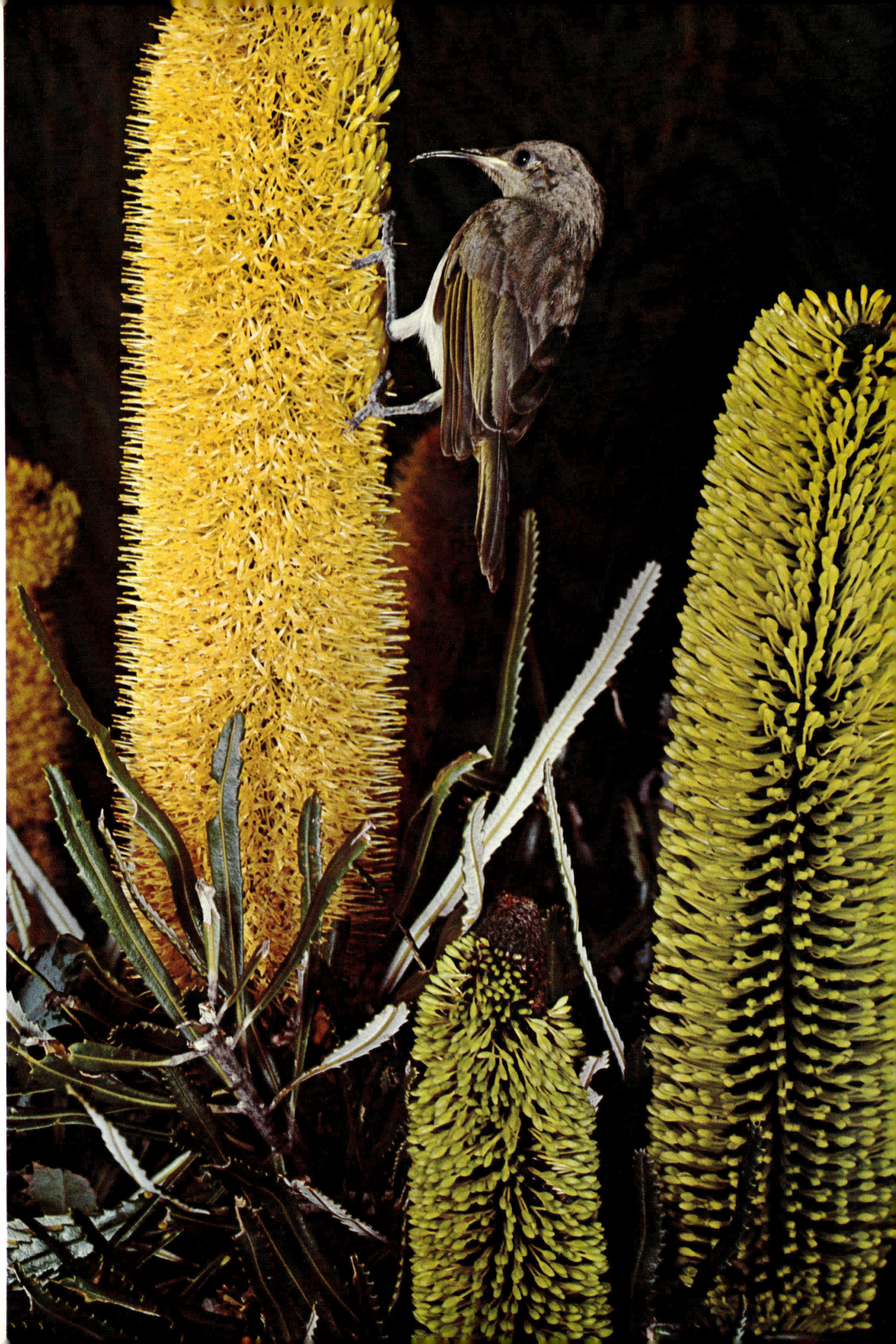

The Brown Honeyeater here perched at the rim of its delicate suspended nest is one of the best of songsters, with powerful, varied notes. This honeyeater, Gliciphila indistincta, is common wherever there are suitable flowers, and is found throughout Australia except in Victoria and South Australia.

Sturt's Desert Pea is to be seen over the interior in a creeping profusion of scarlet and black or, more rarely, with claret-centred flowers. In the wild and in cultivation, these flowers are visited by birds seeking nectar. The long, narrow flowers comprise an upright petal, or standard, and lower petals forming a structure known as the keel. At the junction of keel and standard a narrow slit is the only access to the flower's store of nectar.

When the honeyeater forces its beak into the flower for this nectar, it may perch on, or push against, the lower keel structure, causing the ejection of pollen, pushed out by the plunger movement of the immature style. This pollen may be collected by the honeyeater's plumage, or feet when a small honeyeater stands on the perch-like keel to reach the nectary. When this honeyeater lands at an older flower where the stigma, protruding from the keel, is matured and receptive, the pollen will be effectively transferred. As the pollen is ejected at the distal tip of the keel, it is an inch or more from the nectar source, and so positioned where no insect would need to tread, in its path from flower to flower. One can easily observe this pollen-ejecting action by pressing firmly downward the long scarlet keel of a Sturt Pea flower: the pressure needed is much more than the weight of any insect.

The long racemes of the Bird Flower, *Crotalaria Cunninghamii*, are very similarly constructed, with a closed, slit-like opening which gives to the hard beak of the honeyeater but is closed to insects — bees may be seen investigating these flowers, but do not seem able to force an entry.

Not all birds respect the delicate structures which supply their nectar. Silvereyes have been observed tearing open the long tubes of kangaroo-paws to gain access to nectar otherwise denied to those with such short beaks. Naturally if such methods bypass the anthers, and render many flowers unfit for pollination by their intended pollinator, then the function of the flowers is never achieved and the seed production fails. Should the habit become widespread among these common birds, the future success of this kangaroo-paw could be jeopardized.

Even more than the silvereyes, most honeyeaters are aggressive, active birds, often seen chasing rivals from favoured flowers. If a flower designed perhaps initially for insect pollination, develops a nectar store large enough to become of interest to honeyeaters yet fail to provide easy access for birds, they will easily force a way in, probably damaging the delicate arrangement of parts designed to make insects the pollen carriers. Thus, a flower with significant nectar supply, but closed to birds, would not be permitted to develop but if birds have access to the nectar, then they will be pollinators as well as, or instead of, insects, for the larger flowers.

Among the honeyeaters, which cover the continent wherever there are flowers, there is a great variety in size, colour and song. Some species are almost universal, being found in east and west, many visiting the flowers, native or exotic, in suburban gardens where insecticides — the new, deadly and indiscriminate method of insect control — has not driven out the native birds.

CREATURES OF THE NIGHT

As EACH GLOWING sunset darkens, and daylight colours fade, as shapes of rock and bush and trees slip into gloom but for the branches black against the sky, the world of sight gives way to a world where hearing is the vital sense of hunter and hunted. Even before daylight has faded, night-life is beginning: the kangaroos already feeding, a Boobook Owl calling — perhaps glimpsed in silent flight, a black shape in the darkening sky.

As well as bringing protection for the hunted, nightfall brings coolness for the small creatures of an often hot, and largely arid continent. In the desert-like regions most small reptiles and mammals survive only by avoiding the sun. Their retreats include rock caves or cracks, spinifex, or cooler, humid burrows. With very few exceptions the small marsupials and rodents emerge only at night. By contrast most birds belong to daylight hours, having the powers of flight for escape. Also, being able to reach water from greater distances, birds need not shelter for any reasons of water conservation.

Sight is the vital sense for birds, so it is not surprising that they choose to hunt by day. Among birds only a few predatory forms have developed the refinements needed for flight through the darkness, and for capturing insects and animals which have the protection of darkness. The principal refinement for owls, and no doubt for nightjars and frogmouth, is the development of

The Koala, though sometimes known as "Native Bear", is in fact a completely different animal from any omnivorous placental bear of other lands. The Koala eats only leaves of certain eucalypts, and is a marsupial, bearing tiny young which complete their development in a pouch rather than in the womb. Known scientifically as Phascolarctos cinereus, this animal which is almost the Australian image was brought close to extinction. Careful conservation is now helping koalas extend to suitable areas where they had been wiped out.

About to spring, a five-spring pygmy possum seems to aim its body while gripping leaves with hand-like feet and prehensile tail.

OPPOSITE:

A pygmy possum on a crimson melaleuca seeks nectar, and insects at the flower, after dusk. Hand-like paws make pygmy possums quick among the thinnest twigs, enabling them to hang from a leaf to sample the nectar of a flowering gum, or to leap and land clinging to branch or foliage. The Crimson-flowered Tea-tree, Melaleuca Steedmanii, *is in the same botanical family as the eucalypts. The conspicuous, colourful parts of the flower are the stamens, which in many Australian wildflowers replace petals as the showy part of the flower.*

LEFT:

For this pygmy possum, Cercartetus concinnus, *insects form the main food: any moth or spider or grasshopper to betray its presence by movement is seized, bitten, held up in the forepaws, and daintily eaten — wings and hard parts being discarded. Other* Cercartetus *species inhabit the south east, northern Queensland, and Tasmania.*

In mid-air it spreads its paws wide before making a landing. Slow and sleepy by day, when it is hard to rouse from its hiding place, this miniature marsupial at night moves quickly through the foliage in search of insects, and the nectar of wildflowers.

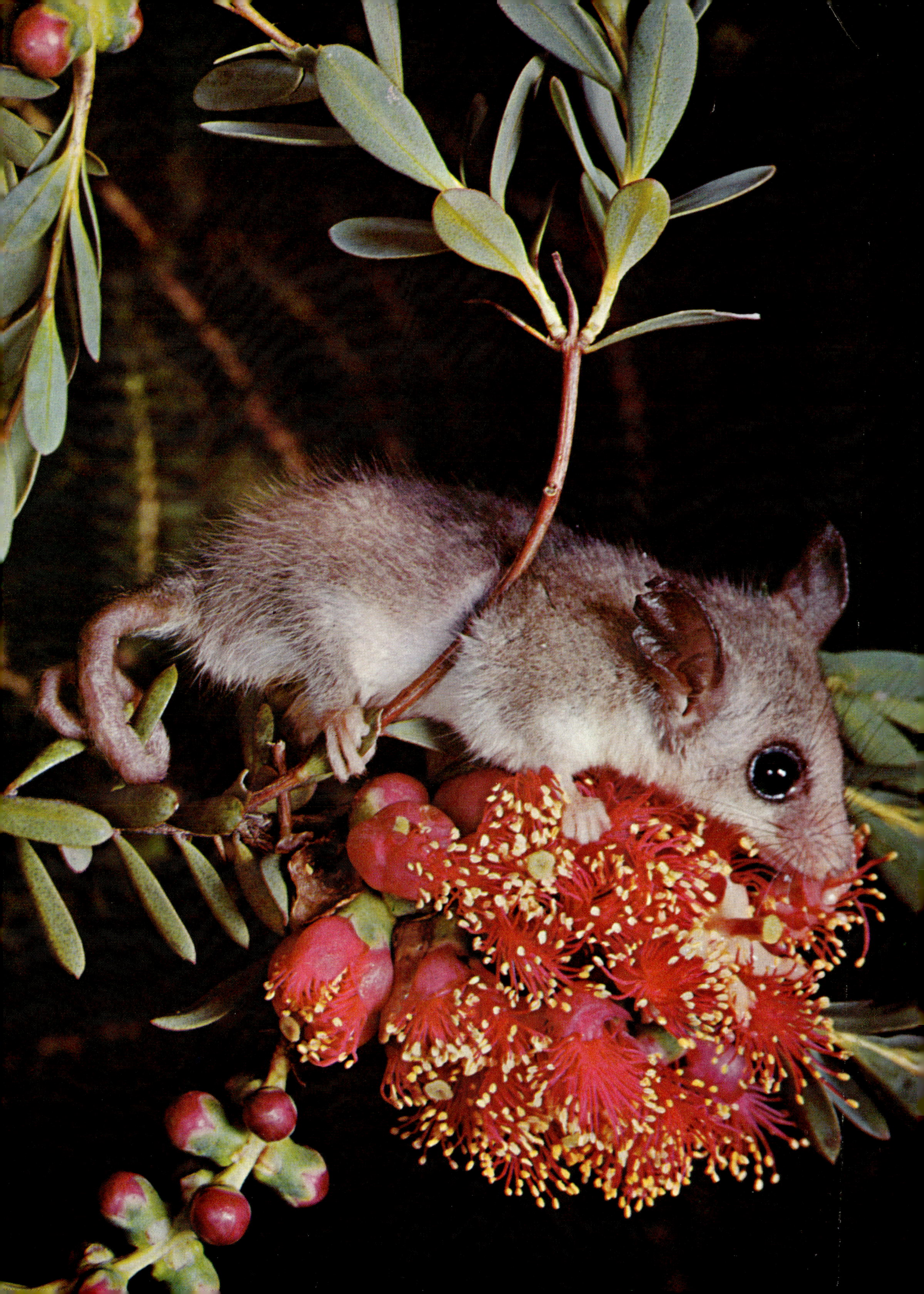

The Grey-headed Fruit Bat, or Flying Fox is one of the world's largest bats, with wingspan reaching four feet. These flying foxes, Pteropus poliocephalus, *at night feed exclusively on fruit, retreating by day to hang in clustered masses in the mangroves of Queensland coastal swamps.*

Leadbeater's Possum, Gymnobelideus leadbeateri, *was long believed extinct until rediscovery in the wet south-eastern forests of Victoria. Though little is known of its habits, it probably feeds on insects and nectar. The long tail is not prehensile, but appears to help maintain balance.*

not only exceptionally keen hearing, but also an accurate directional sound-locating ability.

It has been shown that some owls can strike accurately in total darkness, dropping with claws extended towards any rustling of leaves on the ground. These birds compensate for parallax — the difference in position between guiding ears and striking talons — by bringing the feet up beneath the face while dropping on silent wings towards the prey moving on the ground.

The enormous sensitivity of the ears of owls is suggested by the structure of their eardrums, which in addition to being huge for the size of the bird, vary in size between right and left to assist the pinpointing of sounds in darkness by slight differences in sound intensity. Owls would undoubtedly make use also of the difference of time of arrival of the sound at each ear, for the exact location of prey.

Fine vision is essential for flight itself, so birds' eyes are proportionately large, but even larger again for night-flying birds. Eagles are equipped with eyes of exceptional resolution, able to discern distant detail with ten times the acuity given by the eyes of humans. Owls too have visual acuity greater than night animals like the phalangers, but also share with the small nocturnal mammals, eyes of tremendous light-gathering capacity.

Because the eyes of an owl must be big to gather all available light they are crammed tightly into the orbits or sockets of the skull so that the bird must turn its head to shift the gaze. In fact owls are able to turn their heads in an almost-complete circle.

Among the smallest of the fascinating marsupials — the unique order of Australian pouched* mammals including famous kangaroo and koala — are the tiny Pygmy and Honey Possums, *Cercartetus* and *Tarsipes* scientifically, but also often known by the native names: Mundarda, and Noolbenger.

Though at first glance superficially similar — both being small and roughly mouse-like — closer study reveals real differences. Both feed on the nectar of wildflowers, but while insects are the principal food of the Pygmy Possum, the Honey Possum is so specialized to a nectar diet that its teeth have degenerated over the centuries, till most remain merely as vestigial splints. Its skull has grown long and delicately pointed, its tongue greatly extensile. These adaptations have made it able to exploit the nectar supply of wildflowers which by day support the avian honeyeaters.

* Some without tails.

With the safeguarding help of a long, prehensile tail, the "honey mouse" is able to climb among the thinnest twigs with astonishing speed, and to hang upside down among leaves while reaching flowers. This little marsupial inhabits the banksia, hakea and dryandra scrub of the coastal south-west.

The Pygmy Possum is able to curl completely within the inch-and-a-half wide nest of a Spinebill Honeyeater, or to sit in the bowl of a teaspoon to lick at honey, a favourite food in captivity.

By day this miniature marsupial is slow and drowsy if disturbed, but at sunset throws off daytime lethargy to become a fierce little hunter of insects, and to raid wildflowers of their store of nectar. Hand-like paws with bifid, inflated pads make it quick among the thinnest twigs; enable it to hang from a twig to sample the nectar of a flowering gum, or to leap and land clinging on branch or foliage. Insects provide the main part of Mundarda's diet, so dentally it is better equipped than *Tarsipes*, the Honey Possum. Any moth, spider or insect to betray its presence by movement may be seized, and held in the forepaws while eaten. Within seconds only hard parts remain — discarded wings and legs.

Eyes of the small nocturnal marsupials are black and prominent, seeming to swell out from the head, and no doubt having great light-gathering capacity. When sleeping by day these possums curl tightly into a ball, nose down between forefeet, tail curled over.

Mammals are considered in three broad classes based on reproductive structure. Monotremes include egg-laying Platypus and Spiny Anteater, which have held to the reptilian pattern of the female reproductive organs.

Marsupials include the whole array of Australian pouched animals from kangaroos to possum, bandicoot and phalanger, and some more primitive, pouchless forms. They give birth to tiny young — those of Pygmy and Honey Possums being barely a fifth of an inch long, and the young of the largest kangaroos only an inch long. The tiny "joey", disproportionately formed in that the fore limbs are well developed for climbing, must find its way into its mother's pouch and attach to a nipple to complete its development. Not for some weeks will it show itself at the pouch opening.

The third class is the placental, to which man and all his domesticated animals belong. Most of the mammals of the world are placentals, marsupials being confined almost entirely to Australia.

Placental mode of reproduction is undoubtedly more recent, and is considerably more efficient than the marsupial. It is generally accepted that the more efficient placentals by competition for food and living space caused the extinction of marsupials except in Australia, which was separated from other continents by sea before the evolution of placentals. The replacement of marsupial by placental animal life suggests that the marsupials are inferior to placentals. This implies that the placentals were in competition with marsupials over all continents except Australia, where there were only marsupials and monotremes, and that the placental forms won by virtue of this superiority inherent in the placental plan.

Again, evidence of placental superiority seems to follow from the extinction of many Australian marsupials since the coming of man, while some introduced placentals, notably the rabbit and the fox and the introduced rat, have spread rapidly. But the same situation has arisen for other island

Confined to south-western coastal districts in banksia and bottlebrush scrub, the minute Honey Possum, Tarsipes spenserae, *is a highly specialized nectar feeder with slender muzzle, able to reach into these flowers.*

This small animal is superficially mouse-like in shape and size, but with thicker tail and pointed muzzle, and fierce hunting habits that no mouse ever had. Any small creature is prey and food for these carnivorous marsupials: the Dunnart will tackle spiders, centipedes and small lizards. This species, Sminthopsis crassicaudata, is widely distributed in eastern and in western regions. Similar species inhabit the north. Six to ten young may be born, and carried in the pouch.

LEFT:

Tiny carnivores preying on insects and other small creatures, phascogales are nocturnal hunters now rare in most regions, except Queensland and the Northern Territory. This species, the Red-tailed Phascogale, P. calura, is for most part a denizen of the interior and west; the near-identical Brushtailed Phascogale is the common form in the east and north.

OPPOSITE:

Sensitive eyes, huge and black and with points of light reflecting the flashlight, guide a Boobook Owl emerging from its hollow at night. With silent flight and acute directional hearing, an owl is a capable hunter even in total darkness. This owl, Ninox novae-zeelandiae, calls "boobook": the night sound often described as "mopoke" and attributed to the Tawny Frogmouth — a bird of the Nightjar family.

Rearing upwards, a pugnacious bandicoot displays aggressive tactics which it may often turn on fellow bandicoots encountered at a favoured feeding place. The long sharp claws come into play in fighting, but are mostly used to unearth insects around the roots of plants. Also suited to this mode of life is the pouch in which the female carries her young. With an opening facing to the rear this pouch remains clear of dirt as she scratches around in forest litter and loose soil. The Short-nosed Bandicoot, Isoodon obesulus, is found around the continent while other strange forms, the Rabbit-eared and Pig-footed bandicoots, inhabit the harsher central regions.

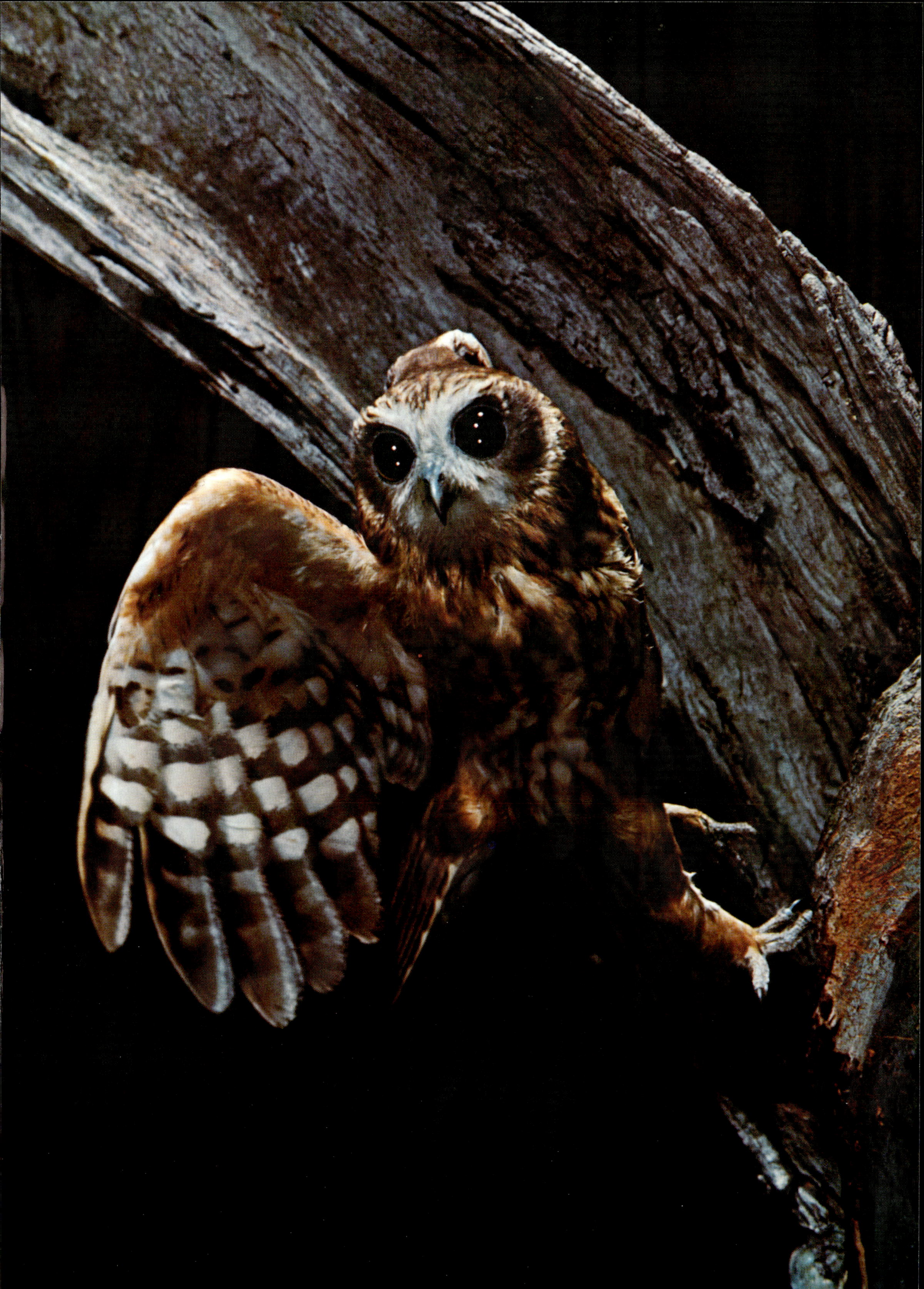

The Feathertail Glider is one of the marsupials with a well-developed membrane for gliding which extends along the flanks and stretches from wrist to elbow. At night these gliders emerge from nests in hollows and glide from tree to tree in search of insects and flowers. Acrobates pygmaeus and its near relatives range from the Northern Territory to South Australia in coastal forest habitat.

populations. The greater part of the West Indies fauna has become extinct since European settlement, and that fauna was entirely placental. There seems a tendency for insular populations, whether marsupial or placental, to decline, often to extinction, in the face of competition from introduced species, and the activities of man. Yet there are always some native species which flourish in the changed environment. Among Australian marsupials the Brush-tailed Possum, ranging across the continent, is adapted to the widest variety of climates and foods and has maintained its numbers despite former wholesale slaughter for skins, and widespread destruction of habitat.

Only rarely do island populations influence continental, so with the Australian fauna insular with respect to the greater continents (which are all more or less interconnected by land bridges)

the form of mammal which has evolved most highly in Australia — the marsupial — could not be expected to influence the continental placentals. But as usual for island populations faced with introduced continental species, much of the Australian animal population has been rendered rare or extinct. With this in mind it has been suggested that the marsupial is not necessarily inferior to any placental evolved for a similar niche.

The Short-nosed Bandicoot, *Isoodon obesulus*, is a species still common in eastern and western States, while other interesting types inhabit the interior and the northern rain forests. Though bandicoots may occasionally be seen scampering through forest undergrowth in broad daylight, they are generally most active after dusk, and seem to rely on an acute sense of smell to locate their prey in soil and forest leaf litter. This prey comprises worms, insects, spiders. Even scorpions and centipedes are seized and devoured with relish. Observers report that such venomous types are dealt with by a rapid scrambling action of the forefeet, which crushes the victim.

Usually the presence of this common species of bandicoot is revealed by small concical pits, scratched out at night in the search for insects. Long sharp claws fit bandicoots for this mode of feeding. The toes of the hind feet show an interesting feature — the second and third toes are fused, or syndactylous. Only at the tips do they separate into two distinct claws. This evolutionary combining of toes is a feature which bandicoots share with the larger well known marsupials, the kangaroos. As well as serving as digging implements, the double toes are believed to function as combs for the harsh, grizzled coat of fur. In dentition — an important basis for animal classification — bandicoots possess an array of sharply pointed incisor teeth like those of the small insect eaters of which the pygmy possum and the dunnart are examples. When fighting the pugnacious bandicoots leap and strike out with long, sharp claws, but in gardens bordering bushland, bandicoot visitors may become quite tame and perform a valuable service in digging out and destroying insects and their larvae.

Ranging in size from a pygmy glider as small as the Pygmy Possum to the Greater Glider larger than the Brushtail Possum, are the phalangers which have evolved gliding forms. Wide membranes of skin from their flanks stretched between wrist and ankle permit long glides by the larger animals, which may sail for a hundred yards or more from a high limb, to land near the base of another tree. Smaller and more primitive pygmy gliders achieve a leap only slightly more prolonged than the unaided jump of the small possums.

Included among phalangers — which all have the opposable big toes enabling them to use hind paws like hands for grasping and climbing — is the unique and famous Koala.

An example of extreme specialization, and living only on the leaves of a few gums, the Koala is one of the most vulnerable and delicate of marsupials. Only sanctuary care has preserved it in the south-east after its earlier widespread destruction by trapping and timber clearing, and by viral or bacterial epidemics.

Like the ground-dwelling wombats and bandicoots, koalas have a backward-facing pouch; an arangement which would appear fatal for the young of any tree-climbing marsupial — but supporting maternal muscles at the pouch opening ensure that suckling baby koalas cannot fall out.

Koalas are believed to have arisen from the same ancestor as the wombat, which it resembles in pouch arrangement, and in solid, stump-tailed appearance: they probably share a common ground-dwelling ancestor which had developed this pouch and tail as most appropriate for a burrowing, earthbound life. Presumably some returned to trees, and though becoming highly specialized in digestive powers for the gum-leaf diet, still retain a smaller, soft and fluffy, wombat shape.

Such modifications are not unusual. A basic feature of evolution is that unused parts, once lost, are never regained, though others may modify to serve the function of the lost part of the anatomy. The koala has never regained the tail which its ancestor presumably lost over the millions of years spent as a wombat-like ground dweller, and it still has an up-side-down pouch.

In all this vast time marsupials have had almost exclusive use of an entire continent, and have experimented with size and form and feature to fill every way of life. Extinct giant marsupials we know only as fossils. Some smaller forms have gone since the coming of man, and many are precariously rare, needing bold and co-ordinated conservation policy for continued survival.

Ringtail possums are forest inhabitants from the Northern Territory and Queensland, through coastal regions to Tasmania, and are also found in the south-western corner. It is hardly surprising that variations occur in a creature distributed from the tropics to cold Tasmanian rainforests: ringtails, Pseudocheirus, have developed eight species, plus further subspecies in which slight but definite differences exist.

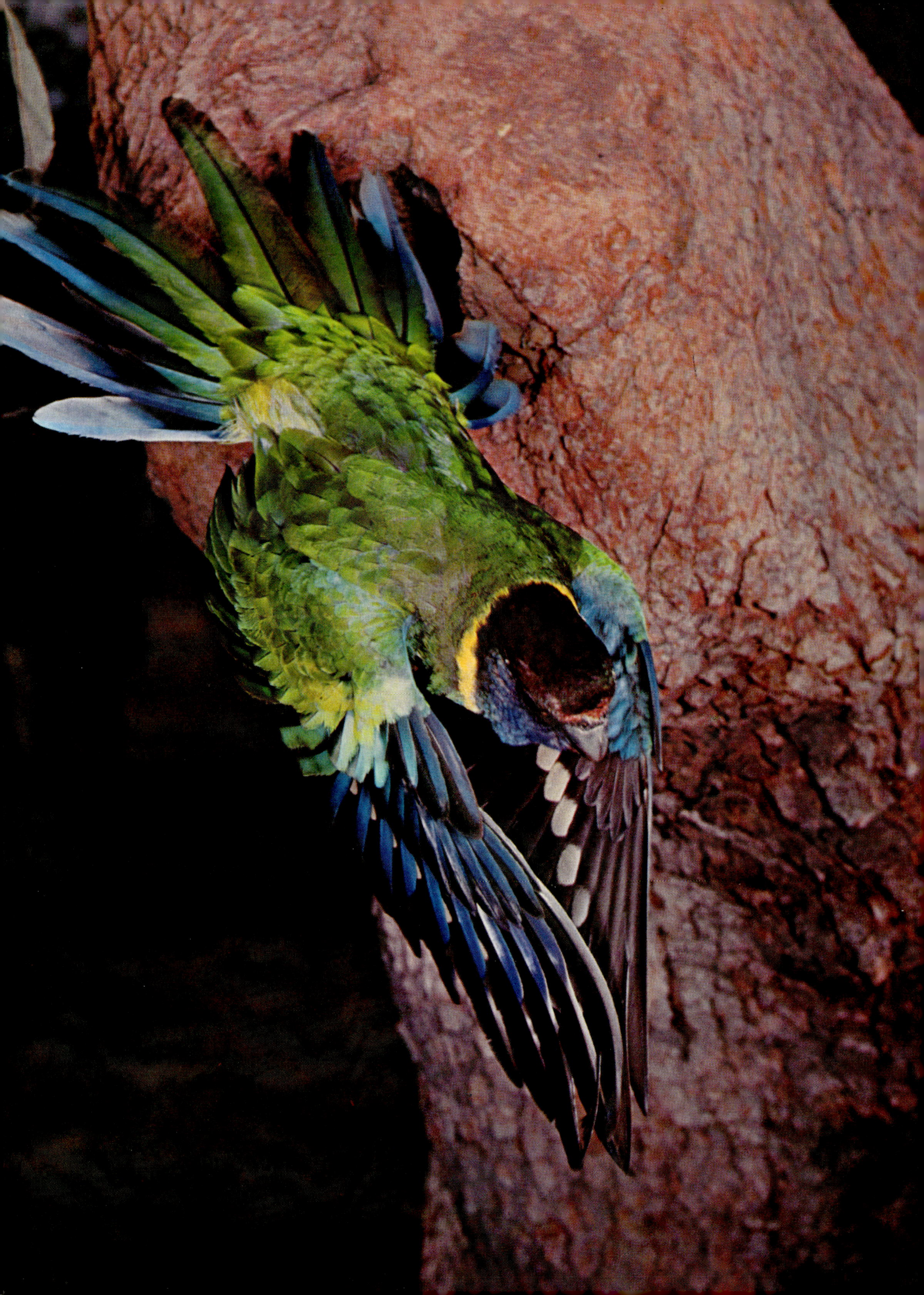

PARROTS, COCKATOOS, LORIKEETS

The australasian region is the headquarters of the *Psittaciformes*; the parrots and cockatoos. Parrots are vastly more numerous in this country than in any other where they occur, and we have many of the most beautiful species.

These birds are highly specialized: their beak shape is well known, with upper mandible permitted to move by means of a transverse hinge attachment to the skull, making possible a powerful action with leverage force greater than in any other birds, enabling parrots to cut through extremely hard objects.

Birds of the parrot family make use of the foot as a hand: toes are paired two forward and two backwards on each foot, enabling them to cling, climb and grasp. As well as making use of the foot as a hand, parrots exhibit abilities of memory and mimicry which, with their magnificent plumage colours make these birds among the best known and most popular of birds; the Australian parrots are valuable aviary subjects throughout the world.

Within the parrot tribe are cockatoos, lorikeets and the parrots. All but one of the seventeen species of cockatoos are birds of the Australasian region, ranging from the giant palm cockatoo of north Queensland, a great black bird with enormous beak and crested head, to the well known white and pink cockatoos of inland plains.

Others include four black species with variously coloured tail bands — from south-western Australia a White-tailed Black Cockatoo, *Calyptorhynchus baudinii*; and in the east a yellow tail species; *C. funereus*, is the common black cockatoo. Through most of Australia may be found the Red-tailed Black Cockatoo. The red-barred tail feathers seen from below with the sun shining through as the big birds land, tail fanned out, in

Diving from its nest hollow, a Twenty-eight Parrot shows spectacular beauty of action and plumage. This parrot is commonly named for its peculiar call: in precise classification it is Barnardius zonarius, *a western form of the Mallee Ringneck, or Port Lincoln Parrot.*

Young rosellas almost ready to fly crowd the narrow opening to the nest hollow in a dead tree. Though just fed by the female several continue to call. The brightly-plumaged male, more timid than his mate, watches from behind the trunk. The Western Rosella, Platycecus icterotis, *is usually a ground-feeding species, taking the seeds of grasses and those fallen from various trees.*

a treetop, glow like fire in the black of the glossy plumage.

Black cockatoos use their powerful beaks in stripping bark in search of insect larvae, and for cutting into hard gum nuts. More brightly plumaged are the pink cockatoos, commonest of which is the Galah, *Kakatoë roseicapilla*, to be seen in vast numbers on inland plains. These flocks present one of the most beautiful spectacles of massed birdlife. Wheeling overhead, sometimes in their hundreds, the Galahs display alternately pink then grey surfaces, in magnificent pattern against the deep-blue sky. Such sights are common, but perhaps more appreciated by visitors to the inland than by Australians who live where these birds are common and persecuted for damage done to crops.

Other cockatoos, unfortunately not as common or as widespread, are the red-headed Gang-gang, from the south east, and the Major Mitchell, or Leadbeater's Cockatoo, *K. leadbeateri*, a magnificent crested bird scattered sparingly across the continent. There are white cockatoos — the Sulphur-crested, and the corellas which feed on the food stores of the ground. With their long upper mandible, Long-billed Corellas dig for roots and bulbs; Little Corellas feed in flocks on the red earth of inland plains and in seemingly-intelligent fashion post sentinels to warn the feeding flock on the ground of danger.

Among parrots Australia has some of the loveliest species. Well known are the rosellas, gaily coloured parrots of many varieties: the Eastern Rosella, the Western Rosella, a Yellow Rosella, Green Rosella, Northern Rosella, and the Pale-headed Rosella. Among their characteristics are the bright cheek patches.

Confined to south-western Australia is a more unusual form of parrot, the Red-capped Parrot, *Purpureicephalus spurius*, which is not only an intensely coloured bird, in contrasting red, green, purple and yellow, but is also interesting as the supposed sole survivor of a form of parrot once widespread in Australia. Now it survives only in a restricted stronghold in the south-west of the continent. The reasons for its extinction over the rest of Australia are not known, though it appears that the long-hooked bill is an adaptation for feeding on the seeds of a certain eucalypt. As the parrot's present distribution coincides with the range of this tree, the Marri, *E. calophylla*, it seems possible that some gradual change in eastern eucalypts may have given the advantage to other parrots, perhaps those of the rosella group, though in the west the Red-cap is able to feed on a variety of foods other than the Marri for which it apparently is specialized. However the seeds of this tree remain a valuable food supply, safe from the attentions of other birds. Whatever factors caused the extinction of this parrot to the east of the desert centre, such factors must have been less or applied more slowly, giving the south-western red-cap population more time to conform to a changing environment. Protection in a habitat separated from the competition of most of the parrots of the rosella group may have helped the red-cap to survive in south-western Australia.

Natural extinction is a necessary and constructive part of evolution: all modes of extinction narrow down to a single cause — a changing environment. In the south-west this balance of nature has in some way shifted in favour of the Red-capped Parrot, making it a common bird, though in the east its ancestral form was unable to survive. In any case, in its western stronghold it seems secure, for though its range is restricted, it is common in the area where the Marri is the principal tree, and one commonly retained on farmland as a useful shade tree.

Seeds of eucalypts are enclosed in a woody fruit, or gum nut, which becomes extremely hard as it matures. The only access to the seeds is through a deep circular opening guarded by a valve structure through which the seeds would eventually be released. While these fruits are immature they are soft and easily chopped open by black cockatoos and the twenty-eight parrots as well as by red-capped parrots. But the hard mature gum nuts hang on the tree for a year or more, the stored seeds then being a valuable food source which only the red-capped parrots can exploit by prying out the seeds through the narrow valves with the lengthened hook on the upper beak. Other parrots and cockatoos are confined to green gum nuts for the few months of the year when they are relatively soft.

Adaptive forces of evolution show again in the ring-neck parrots, but in plumage colour change rather than beak structure. In former ages, central regions of Australia were less arid than at present, and allowed some of the fauna to extend in unbroken distribution from east to west. Among these must have been the green and yellow plumaged ring-neck parrots — the various *Barnardius* species. In some subsequent arid age an expanding desert heart cut apart the eastern and western populations of this parrot, so that each group developed independently according to the environment of its region. Those isolated in south-western forests became greener, and lost the yellow breast. Despite the colour difference these had not become separate species, but had gone no further than becoming varieties of the one species. When a further swing of the long climatic cycle brought another age of less arid conditions to the Australian centre, a second invasion of the yellow-breasted parrots reached the south-west, to interbreed with the easternmost of the all-green ring-necks, so that now the twenty-eights shade from green birds of coastal forests, which have the call sounding like the words "twenty-eight", to a yellow-fronted population in drier inland, eastern parts, the latter being the bird known in South Australia as the Port Lincoln Parrot, but being separated from the eastern port lincolns by the now desert Nullabor Plains.

Through the open scrubland and among the river gums of inland watercourses may be found the multi-coloured Mulga Parrot, *Psephotus varius*, one of a group of bright little parrots whose distinctive plumages are briefly indicated in the names — Blue Bonnet, Red-backed, Golden-shouldered, and Paradise.

Like the mulga parrots, others of the family have become exclusively birds of the desert and its semi-arid fringes. The rather rare Bourke Parrot, *Neophema bourkii* (now reported as increasing in numbers in some districts), the extremely rare Scarlet-chested Parrot *Neophema splendida*, and the common and well-known Budgerigar are but a few.

Small honeyeaters and insectivorous birds of dry regions may survive with little water except the heavy inland dews, but finches and parrots dependent upon dry seed food must visit the waterholes to drink; the commoner birds in great flocks at sunrise, and again in the evening.

Lorikeets, small nectar-eating parrots predominantly green but splashed with crimson, orange, purple and blue, exploit the vast eucalyptus forests. Wandering from region to region with the flowering of these trees, the lorikeets crush

The female rosella pauses while feeding her five young. Food is given by regurgitation of seeds collected in two or three hours of ground foraging. In the trunk five or six feet below this opening her eggs were deposited on bare wood dust and debris. Now the fully-feathered young in their eagerness climb in the hollow to the opening, when the adults approach and call.

flowers with their short parrot beaks to take the nectar with brush-tipped tongues. Lorikeets include the smallest of Australian parrots. The Purple-crowned Lorikeet, *Glossopsitta porphyrocephala*, is barely six inches long, and among the smallest of Australian parrots. These lorikeets may be seen among the stunted flowering mallees of inland sandplains, among the cream-flowered trees of the Wandoo forests (where they were photographed in August) and in mid-summer be heard screeching high in the crowns of tall Karris, where they nest again, prompted by the wealth of the honey flow of the flowering forest giants.

Most Australian parrots nest in hollows of trees, exceptions being the Paradise Parrot (now rendered almost extinct in the wild by the activities of those who trap birds for sale) which nested in the large mounds of termites in the north; and the Rock Parrot, which lays its eggs in a crevice or hollow of coastal limestone in a site often dashed by ocean spray in rough weather. The rare Ground Parrot and Night Parrot nest in hollows scratched out under low vegetation.

Parrots and cockatoos lay white eggs, which are placed on the bare wood inside a tree hollow; and the incubating female is usually fed by the male. These noisy and affectionate birds maintain their pair bonds for years, often returning annually to the same hollow to nest.

A Port Lincoln Parrot rushing from its hollow displays the yellow undersurface which differentiates it from the green-breasted Twenty-eight. Otherwise, both Barnardius species are very similar, so that some authorities classify each as separate; others consider them only as different geographical races of one species. The Port Lincoln form, Barnardius barnardi, *is distributed through low rainfall areas of eastern Australia, while in Western Australia it is inland of the forest habitat of the Twenty-eight Parrot.*

Nesting in late spring months when the hot November sun has browned the grass of distant fields, a richly plumaged male Redcap throws wings wide and twists for sudden take-off. The young parrot he has just fed looks from the hollow, appearing well-feathered and almost ready to fly. A strongly hooked bill enables these parrots to pry seeds from the hard woody capsules of the Marri, a common eucalypt of their south-west habitat. Red-capped Parrots, Purpureicephalus spurius, *are found only in the south-western corner of Australia. Nests are invariably high. In colour the female is similar, but just lacks the intensity of hues seen in the plumage of the male.*

OPPOSITE:

Diving from its nest hollow in the weathered, knotted wood of an old gum, this Galah gives a glimpse of the grace and beauty of a bird which is one of the commonest of inland Australia. In the hollow the Galah, Kakatoë roseicapilla, *may lay five round white eggs on a lining of fresh gumleaves, and two broods may be raised in favourable seasons. Aided by land clearing and provision of water, these graceful birds have extended their range on both sides of the continent.*

Against a background of a beautiful desert river winding between steep red-rock banks, a vivid Mulga Parrot lands at the hollow which is its nest. Stunted mulga scrub of the interior affords few sites for the larger birds, which come to nest in the river gums. This parrot, Psephotus varius, *is also called "Many-coloured Parrot".*

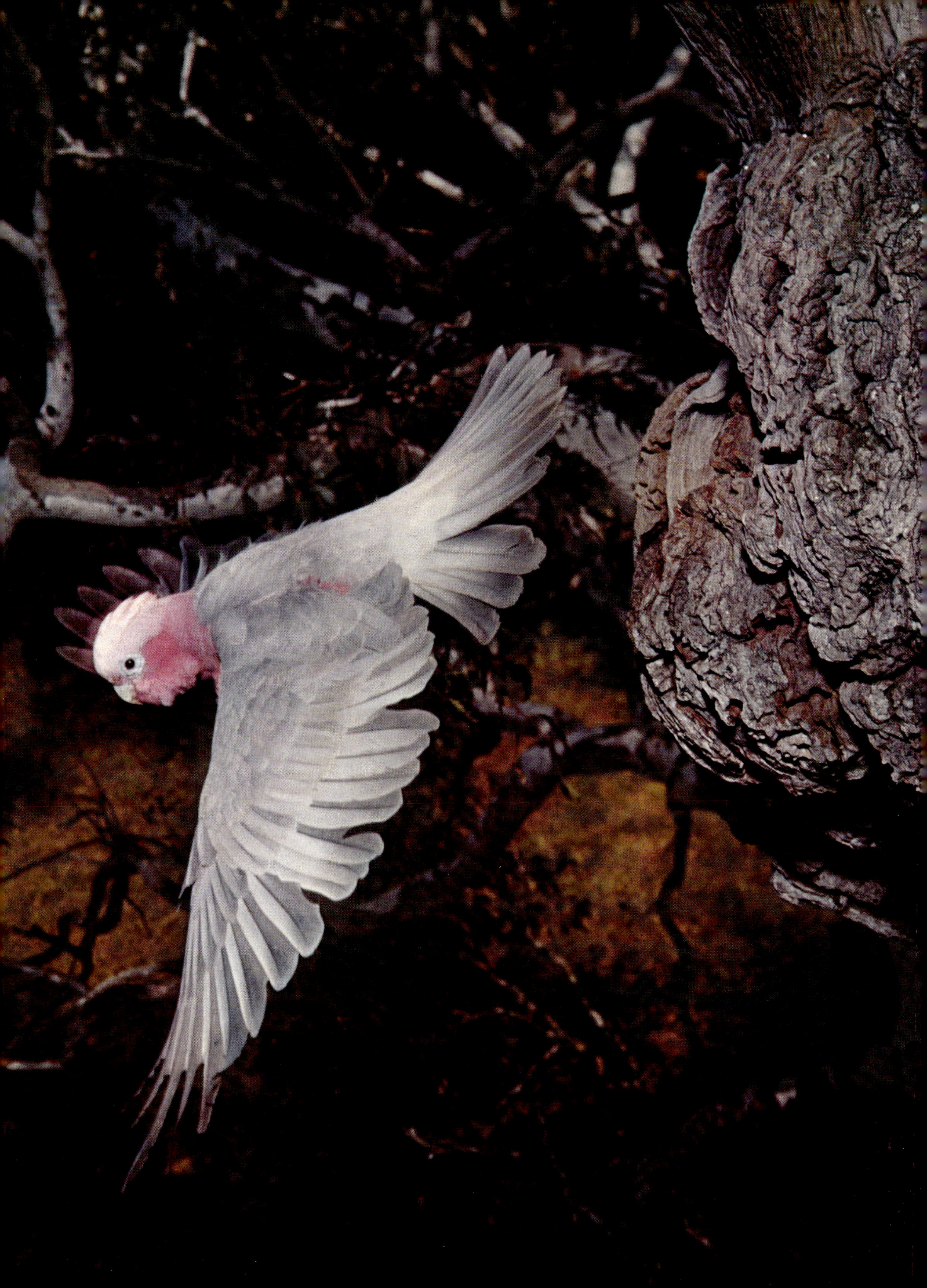

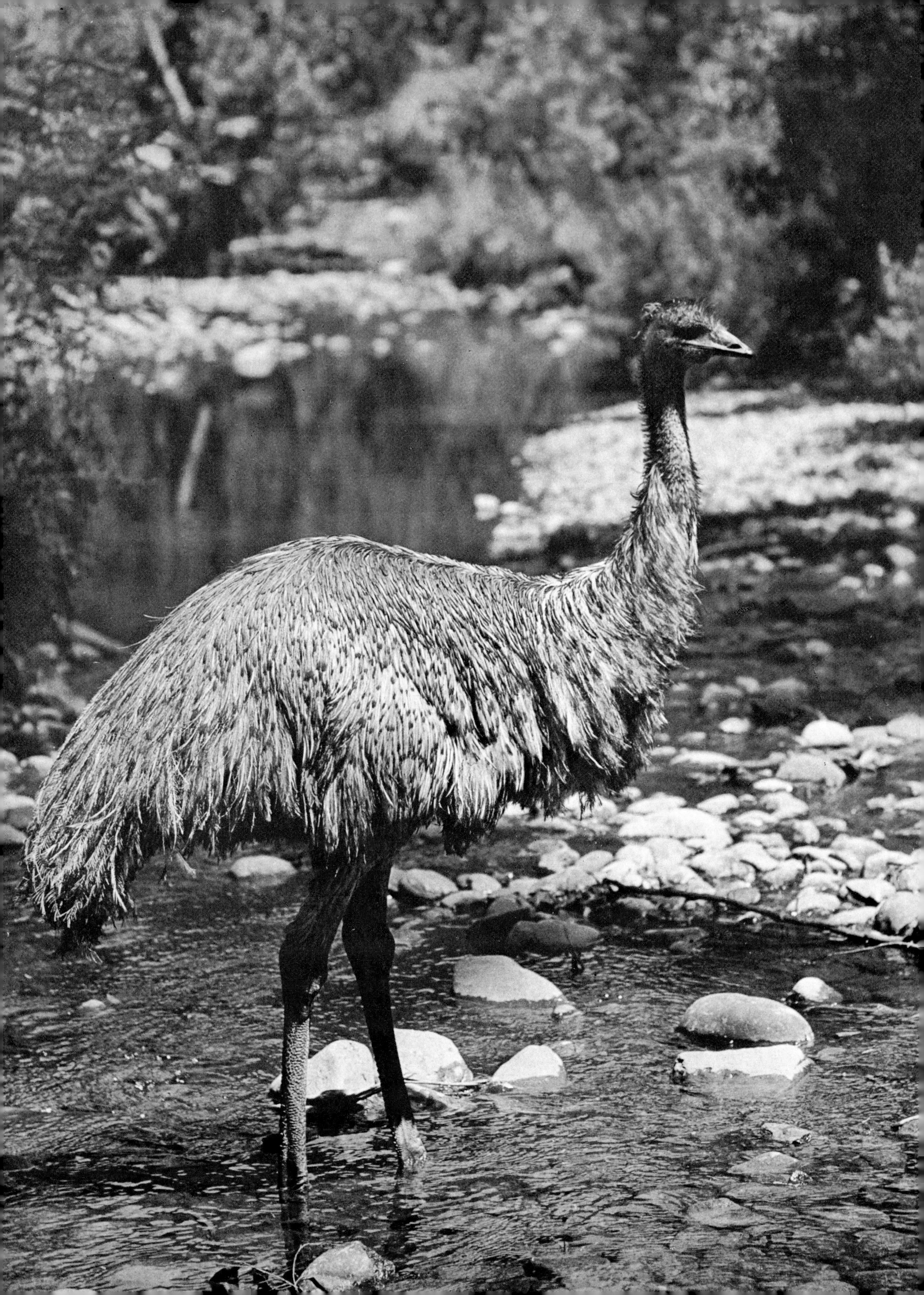

THE ARID LANDS

DUNES, SALTPANS, shimmering gibber-stone plains, cruel spinifex, swirling red dust: these are terms which might usually express impressions of a desert and which could build a picture of Australia's arid interior at its worst. But the vast regions lumped together under such terms as "dead heart", "barren interior", or "outback" are not always so grim. The greater part of the dry region of Australia is thickly vegetated with growth ranging from the solid river gums along inland watercourses and ghost gums scattered where occasional storm water runs from rocky hills, to the harsh mulga scrub, and the pungent-pointed spinifex.

After rare heavy rains the bare earth beneath mulga scrub becomes a carpet of white, gold, pink and purple as the transient annuals rush through their short lives — a pageantry lasting but a few weeks. Soon only withered stems remain, but in the red dust lie the hard seeds of the next generation. These are the "everlastings", with dry papery petals that retain colour and shape without water for weeks after picking.

When tropical cyclones swing in from the northern seas, with their sudden torrential rains filling the dry, rocky watercourses and flooding the sandy dry rivers miles wide in places, it is not only plant life that flourishes. With these irregular "once in a while" rains, which may bring inches in a few hours just once or twice in a year or two,

One of the world's largest living bird species, the Emu (Dromaius novae-hollandiae — the "swift-footed bird of New Holland") has remained common over much of inland Australia. On rough but open country its speed, and toughness under the protecting mass of feathers combine to protect it from most dangers. Emus roam the plains in small mobs, finding a living in the poorest of arid country, but seek shelter of thicker scrub when nesting. The huge eggs require more than two months' incubation — a long task always undertaken by the male.

The Dingo, Canis dingo, is of the same stock as domestic dogs, but yelps and howls instead of barking. The earliest dingo remains certainly dated, go back but a short time in the history of this ancient continent — perhaps some three to six thousands years, so the Dingo is a relative newcomer to the continent, probably introduced by Aborigines as a half-domestic dog. Running wild, it was probably responsible for the extinction of the Tasmanian Tiger and Devil on the mainland.

After good rains in the dry inland—a thunderstorm, or cyclone swinging in from northern seas — the Sturt Desert Peas, Clianthus formosus, *spread as vines, carpeting the red desert clay with green, then bursting into flower, all within a few weeks. Spreading until the ground dries to its familiar hardbaked, hostile state: then the crimson pea and all the other transient flowers wither and die. Usually the Sturt Pea has a black centre; more rarely this deep claret appears.*

A Wedgebill with sombre plumage matching the harsh scrub gathers together the blue shells, and stands for a moment watching the helpless things in her nest. These bright shells were dropped where they would attract no predator, away from the nest, before she and her mate, clad in the same brown plumage, returned with the first small insects. Wedgebills have a clear, ventriloquial song: notes sadly beautiful and in keeping with the rigours of the desert; ringing louder and louder on all sides, though the singer seems always hidden.

For hundreds of miles the land beyond the tree-lined river is flat and dry, clad only in stunted mulga or patches of harsh spinifex — but transformed in spring by a profusion of wildflowers if rain has fallen. Birds come to these river gums to nest. Noisy, colourful parrots and cockatoos, together with bright little finches, robins and honeyeaters make each inland river a wildlife wonderland. Here the Ashburton River cuts deep through northwestern plains, yet may flood miles wide over these high banks when occasional cyclonic rains reach inland.

Though statistically averaging five or ten inches of rain a year, most parts of the interior may get a few really wet days only once or twice in a year or two, filling the saltpans and flooding the rivers — but for every wet day there are months of clear skies, searing sun, and hot dry winds.

One of the smallest of birds, and bearing long tail plumes of emu-feather pattern, Rufous-crowned Emu-wrens live and nest among the hard grass of spinifex clumps. They are widely distributed through the interior from north-west to central north, but usually hard to find or to glimpse for more than a moment.

Geckos, Gehyra variegata, *and other insect eaters survive arid conditions because they get water in their prey. Most small creatures avoid extreme heat in burrows or under rock slabs.*

the desert frogs appear. Responding immediately to the moisture, they struggle upwards from their protective clay chambers as the dry cracked mud softens to the rare touch of water.

These desert frogs cram a life cycle into a few short weeks when water fills the claypans. The mechanism varies. The eggs of some species undergo extremely rapid development allowing the tadpoles to complete their metamorphosis to the air-breathing form before the pools dry out. For the long, waterless periods that pervade most inland climates of Australia, frogs have adapted themselves by avoiding the dangerously dry situation.

The shortness of the wet periods poses problems for creatures so dependent upon dampness not only for the requirements of a skin which must stay moist, but also for the breeding and tadpole stages of the life cycle. For the desert frogs, falling rain is an immediate breeding stimulus.

Some lay their eggs in wet burrows, where development proceeds in the normal way except that the tadpole remains within the egg until it has reached an advanced state, for if it hatched under the dry conditions, dessication and death would follow. With the next heavy rains these eggs are flooded out and washed to a pool where the tadpoles hatch and complete their metamorphosis.

Some, like *Cyclorana platycephalus*, the Waterholding Frog, survive the long drought between rains by burrowing with a store of water in the body, so that as the mud dries out the frog survives encased in hardened clay—a tiny chamber wherein the vital condition of dampness can be maintained.

Although frogs must obviously adapt greatly in development and in behaviour to minimize the great dangers which a desert environment must impose for an amphibian, other creatures must also adapt their ecology to the demands of such a rigorous habitat.

The reptile fauna of the Australian desert is rich and varied. Most groups of reptiles found in Australia have representatives living in the central arid regions. Deserving distinction for sheer size is the Perentie, *Varanus giganteus*, which grows to eight feet or more in length, but there are also the delicate geckoes, fast-moving dragons, the brightly-patterned skinks, and the scale-footed or legless lizards.

Although the Australian snakes include some deadly species—the squat death-adders and the fast, venomous brown snakes, there are also the small, colourful species with bright rings or patterns around the body.

Many of these lesser snakes burrow rapidly in the sand, some being blind, small and wormlike, and feeding mainly on termites and insects. The Little Whip Snake, often found under logs and

A legless lizard, Delma fraseri, *with protruding scales the only external sign of vanished legs. These vestigial legs are too small to show here, but clearly visible are external ear openings which snakes do not have.*

debris, is a widespread beneficial species which appears to have a preference for termites.

A dry-country reptile of remarkable appearance is the Mountain Devil, a slow-moving dragon lizard which feeds entirely on ants, of which a thousand may be consumed at a meal. It is also reputed to change colour to match its surroundings. At least it is able to fade or brighten the colours. The colour pattern persists, but merely becomes more or less obvious as the case may be, as the integumentary background pales or darkens. This is sufficient to transform it from a bright orange-yellow, black patterned to resemble a stony red-earth habitat, to dull grey-black, more like granite rocks and soil.

Reptiles were the first vertebrate form of life to develop towards elimination of water as the limiting factor in distribution. Consequently the group contains many of the most successful desert adaptations. Water may come from the bodies of their prey, while conservation of water, and protection from extreme heat is often accomplished by burrowing, for the temperature below the surface may be ten degrees cooler than the sun-baked surface. Rock crevices and spinifex clumps are shelter for others.

Absorption through the skin is a water source for some species — it has been reported often for the Mountain Devil — and may allow entry and utilization of water brushed onto the body from dew-damped grass and stones. Heavy dews are an almost nightly occurrence of inland parts, and must be a valuable water source for the smaller creatures.

Larger desert animals also show patterns of behaviour developed to avoid extreme heat and water loss. The Euro and the Red Kangaroo "lie-up" by day in rocky caves of breakaway country, or under dense scrub, avoiding unnecessary action during the hottest hours. These and other large kangaroos and wallabies use water for cooling, but in dry country cannot afford to use much water in this way: they lick the fur of forearms and chest, but this is relatively inefficient.

The Red Kangaroo, Macropus rufus, *is the largest of the marsupials. By day it lies up, avoiding the heat in the shade of trees or bushes, and appearing in large mobs at dusk on open plains. The female is often a contrasting blue-grey, and called the "blue flyer". Though kangaroos bound on long hind legs at speed, their slow walk involves supporting action of forefeet and tail which support the animal tripod fashion as the hind legs are brought forward.*

Although alarming in appearance, the Mountain Devil, Moloch horridus, *is quite harmless; a slow-moving eater of ants. It is able to change the intensity of its colours; to fade and darken parts of the pattern and blend with surroundings.* Moloch *is often reported to drink through its skin — perhaps a way of utilizing the heavy nightly dew of these regions. This would be a development of real survival value in desert country.*

In addition to several large and very dangerous snakes, Australia has also a number of small and often colourful species, like this Little Whip Snake, Denisonia gouldii, *which feeds principally on termites, and though venomous, is not dangerous.*

A common, but always beautiful sight through vast inland regions, is the Galah. Whether seen as a solitary splash of pink and grey against the blue, or in great flocks which circle in unison, showing alternately massed pink undersurfaces, then their silver-grey backs, before settling on the ground to feed.

The Australian Little Eagle may not be big when compared perhaps with the majestic black wedgetail, but has true eagle character with fully 'trousered' legs and solid form. This eagle, Hieraaëtus morphnoides, *occurs in this attractive light phase, with pure white under parts delicately flecked with rust red streaks; and also in a darker form. It is an inland bird which in recent years has extended coastwards, preying principally on rabbits. An egg can just be seen in the nest, and under the talons of the eagle are the remains of a rabbit.*

Downy young eagles may wait hours between parental visits as they grow older. When they were small the female would stay at the nest, sheltering them, or tearing apart the prey, and offering small pieces of meat on the tip of her beak.

For greater cooling effect evaporation should be from the skin surface. They must drink water to make up the loss, but manage with drinks at long intervals.

Smaller desert mammals cannot afford the water loss resulting from cooling by evaporation. Their survival tactics are behavioural rather than physiological: they avoid the most severe heat stresses by nocturnal hunting. In their burrows beneath scrub or spinifex the day temperatures are lower, the humidity higher.

Extreme among the marsupials which burrow, and possibly most adapted of all to desert conditions, is the small, blind Marsupial Mole, *Notoryctes typhlops*, which lives in the sand-ridged country, and emerges only after wet weather.

In contrast with desert amphibians, reptiles and mammals, the birds of arid regions have few special adaptations for water and temperature control. By flight they are able to cover considerable distances to water several times a day. It is well known that increased bird life in the desert means water near at hand. Flocks of parrots and cockatoos can lead to water if followed in the morning or evening. These eaters of dry seeds must seek water daily, but small insectivorous birds may survive on the liquid in the bodies of their victims for longer periods, but plentiful insect life extends over the most barren regions only after rain.

Like other desert life, most birds avoid activity during the hottest hours. The half-light just before dawn is heralded with the noisy activity of birdlife, which gradually subsides after sunrise as the temperature climbs towards and past the century.

Few birds are active in the heat of the day: bee-eaters, perhaps, or eagles which can create their own micro-climate by soaring to heights where the air is cooler.

Desert birds are quick to seize the opportunity to breed under favourable conditions when rain falls. This is a characteristic of very great survival value in the hostile environment. It has been shown that the lower the average annual rainfall of a region, the quicker its birds are to take advantage of suddenly-improved conditions for breeding. Some begin courtship displays and nest-building almost as the rain begins to fall, others wait for the first green grass. One of the most successful among such opportunist breeders is the Grey Teal, which is 'triggered' to nest with rising water levels in claypans and swamps, but in fact few birds of arid places do not breed in response to rain.

In coastal districts favoured with regular winter rainfall, spring nesting is the pattern. Inland birds

Though the Nankeen Kestrel, smallest of our birds of prey, usually confines itself to grasshoppers, lizards, mice and the like, this bird flying into its nest hollow carries part of some larger prey — perhaps the young of some ground-nesting bird. The Kestrel, Falco cenchroides, is widespread in the desert, where it nests in holes in the cliffs of breakaway country, and even in the underground caverns of the Nullarbor Plain.

The alarming combination of expanded frill, and loud hiss exuding from wide, bright yellow mouth is a most effective deterrent to most enemies of a Frilled Lizard. A three-foot dragon lizard, Chlamydosaurus kingii, *has a wide range in the tropical north, from Queensland to the Kimberlies.*

which have abandoned regular spring nesting to respond to rain at any time of the year include Rufous-crowned Emu-wren, Blue-and-white Wren, Variegated Wren, Wedgebill, and many others. The birds of prey — Kestrel, Australian Little Eagle, and the great Wedgetail Eagle have chosen, as has the Emu, to ignore the lush conditions after the rare good rains, and to hold fast to old habits of unvaried spring nesting.

The Australian flora is without parallel for its adaptation to an arid climate. Though some desert trees, like the Baobab, with its water-storage trunk have made massive adaptation, most Australian plants have adapted to the rigours of the climate by equally-important, though less conspicuous means. Whereas bird and animal life can, to some

Silvered twigs and gum nuts of a small eucalypt add decorative charm throughout the year; through winter months it carries masses of pendant pink flowers. This tree, Eucalyptus caesia, is popularly known by the native name, "Gungurru".

RIGHT:

The Corkwood, Hakea lorea, is a tree of the desert: scattered across arid spinifex plains it is often the only large form of vegetation. Rough-barked and stunted, this hakea has in long, pendulous racemes of flowers as its greatest claim to beauty.

The Flame Grevillea, Grevillea excelsior, holds long orange spikes high on slender bare stems above the grey-green, pine-like foliage, where they become a feature of western sandplain landscapes.

After rare heavy rains the bare earth beneath mulga scrub becomes carpeted with the white, gold, pink, and purple of the transient annuals. The pageantry lasts but a few weeks. Soon the earth is dry again; only the withered stems and scattered papery flowers remain of these bright "everlastings". But in the dust lie the hard seeds which can survive drought and scorching heat, and will again brighten the desert with colour.

Flowering in summer, and standing close-packed on three-foot stems, this Golden Feather Flower covers sandy western flats with gold brighter than any field of ripened wheat, and extends over acres, beneath scattered banksia trees. Feathery flowers in a mushroom crown hide the foliage beneath their dense layer. Verticordia nitens may spring almost to full height in a year, then each summer form a new floral crown just an inch or two above the old.

extent, evade the greatest extremes of heat and dessication, plants must remain bound within limitations of soil moisture, so that their adaptations to aridity must necessarily be more thorough

Much of inland Australia is covered by hardy *Acacia*, well adapted to the harshness of the habitat. This mulga covers probably a greater part of Australia than any other vegetation type. The term "mulga" may be applied as a vernacular name for one wattle species, *Acacia aneura*, or used to describe vast regions where various acacias, low, straggling, sparsely foliated and often thorny, are the predominant vegetation. Mulga bridges the gap between the hardiest eucalypts and the true desert vegetation where bushes become more and more widely scattered, until completely replaced by spinifex, saltbush, bare gibber-stone plains, and sand-dunes.

Acacias of the mulga regions flower quickly after rain, unlike their spring-flowering coastal relatives. Their hard seeds can lie on the hard-baked soil for years, but still germinate when rain eventually comes.

Among other survival techniques of desert trees and shrubs may be listed deep taproots, reduced leaf area, and a felted or powdery covering to foliage and stems, designed to reduce water loss by transpiration when hot dry winds are blowing.

Of greatest interest to the tourist is the wealth of the ephemeral flora of this mulga country. Beneath the widely-spaced shrubs in spring the hard red clay is hidden by carpeting "everlastings" — papery-flowered, herbaceous plants of the *Compositae*: the pink, white and gold of *Helipterum*, *Helichrysum*, and of *Cephalipterum Drummondii*.

More favoured in rainfall are the "mallee" regions, which are generally spread between the mulga scrub and the taller eucalypts of the more humid coastal belts. Like "mulga", "mallee" refers either to a single shrub, or to an area, in this case dominated by stunted eucalypts, which have the common characteristic of suckering profusely from a bulbous root stock, particularly following damage or destruction of the main stem by wind or fire.

Fire has long been an element of this environment, started in the past by the Aborigines to drive out game, and by lightning. Its effect on the flora varies from species to species, but all have survived to adapt: some, like the mallee eucalypts, certain banksias, and verticordias sucker out with many new stems at the base. Other species may be killed, but regenerate rapidly from seed. It is the ability of seeds to withstand fire that is one of the most valuable adaptations of this flora. In a few species, fire even seems an essential prerequisite for germination.

Banksias retain their large, winged seeds for years on the tree in unopened follicles of solid woody structure, which the transient heat of fire will open. But the seeds do not immediately glide into the flames — the buffeting of wind is needed to shake them from horizontal slits.

Other natives, the hakeas, callistemnons, and the eucalypts have hard, thick-walled seeds which crack slightly after heating, and which often are not released until the death of branch or whole of the parent plant.

Through the mallee and mulga country the Australian interior is seldom without life and vegetation. Even the most barren parts have occasional trees. Ghost Gums, and the golden-flowered Corkwoods, *Hakea laurina*, shelter in depressions and below rocky hills even in the stony and sandy deserts otherwise with no large vegetation: there a little water collects after any rare storm, and there each clump of the ubiquitous *Triodia* shelters its community of small creatures.

BIRDS BENEATH THE GROUND

Although deserving distinction for plumage alone, in a land of beautiful birds, several species have an added distinction: they nest beneath the ground. For some reason, certain brightly coloured birds, which for most of the year will be seen only in the treetops among fresh green foliage, or hawking insects above, dig into the ground which they might never otherwise touch. There they nest and rear young in the dank, dusty darkness of a subterranean chamber.

The Rainbow Bird, or Bee-eater, is of a large group, the order *Coraciformes*, whose members — including bee-eaters, kingfishers, and the woodpeckers, all nest in hollows of trees or the ground. The Spotted Diamond Bird, however, is not only a member of the order of song birds (*Passeriformes*) among which elaborately constructed nests are common, but also appears formerly to have constructed a nest in the foliage of trees or shrubs. Pardalotes still construct nests, but of bark strips in an underground chamber or, in the case of the Red-tipped Pardalote, in a small hollow of a tree.

The Spotted Diamond Bird, or Pardalote, now constructs its domed bark nest at the end of a short tunnel which may be drilled into a creek bank beneath overhanging vegetation, or hidden between mossy boulders on the forest floor. So small and well-hidden is the entrance, that the nest would usually remain undetected but for the frequent visits of the birds.

The Spotted Pardalote may have chosen to build in a tunnel for the security offered by such an enclosed site, or because subterranean temperatures are more constant, and warmer than outside

With wings unfolding for flight, a Little Bat, Eptesicus pumilis, *clambers from the mud nest of a fairy martin, where it sheltered in daylight hours. This is one of the commoner bats, found in east and west. It does not live in large colonies.*

Rainbow Birds, also called Bee-eaters, feed exclusively upon insects caught in flight: dragonflies on occasions, but more commonly marchflies, and bees, which are efficiently rendered harmless. A systematic series of operations ensure that the lethal sting is destroyed. The preliminary whack of bee against branch serves to determine which is the head and which the soft sting end. Then the sting is rubbed repeatedly against the perch, usually with the result that the entire sting remains on the branch. A vigorous head-whacking precedes the final despatch of the bee. Remarkably, insects of similar size, but not possessing the bee's formidable weapon, are treated only the killing blows without any preceding 'de-stinging'.

Eggs of the rainbow bird lie on bare earth among debris of insect fragments. The chamber is usually connected to the outside world by a gently sloping three-foot tunnel. Nesting is in summer months, when the subterranean chamber maintains a more humid and uniform warmth than the outside air — a factor in favour of an underground nest.

LEFT:
The newly-hatched are quickly able to shuffle around the confines of the chamber. They seem able to distinguish light and dark, though eyes are unopened, for all huddle together in the darkest corner most of the time.

OPPOSITE:
As one rainbow bird glides down with a captured insect, its mate backs from the nest tunnel. From favoured perches, roadside wires or dead branches over forest clearings, rainbow birds, Merops ornatus, *dart out to chase in twisting, turning flight, each passing bee or dragonfly.*

An adult coming through the tunnel darkens the chamber, and the young soon learn to recognize this as the sign of approaching food. Still unable to see, they mill about excitedly. Developing feathers fail to hide their grotesque form, for each feather is enclosed in a protective sheath of wax, so that each little bee-eater gets a coat of spines. When the sheaths eventually split away, the feathers are revealed in full adult colours.

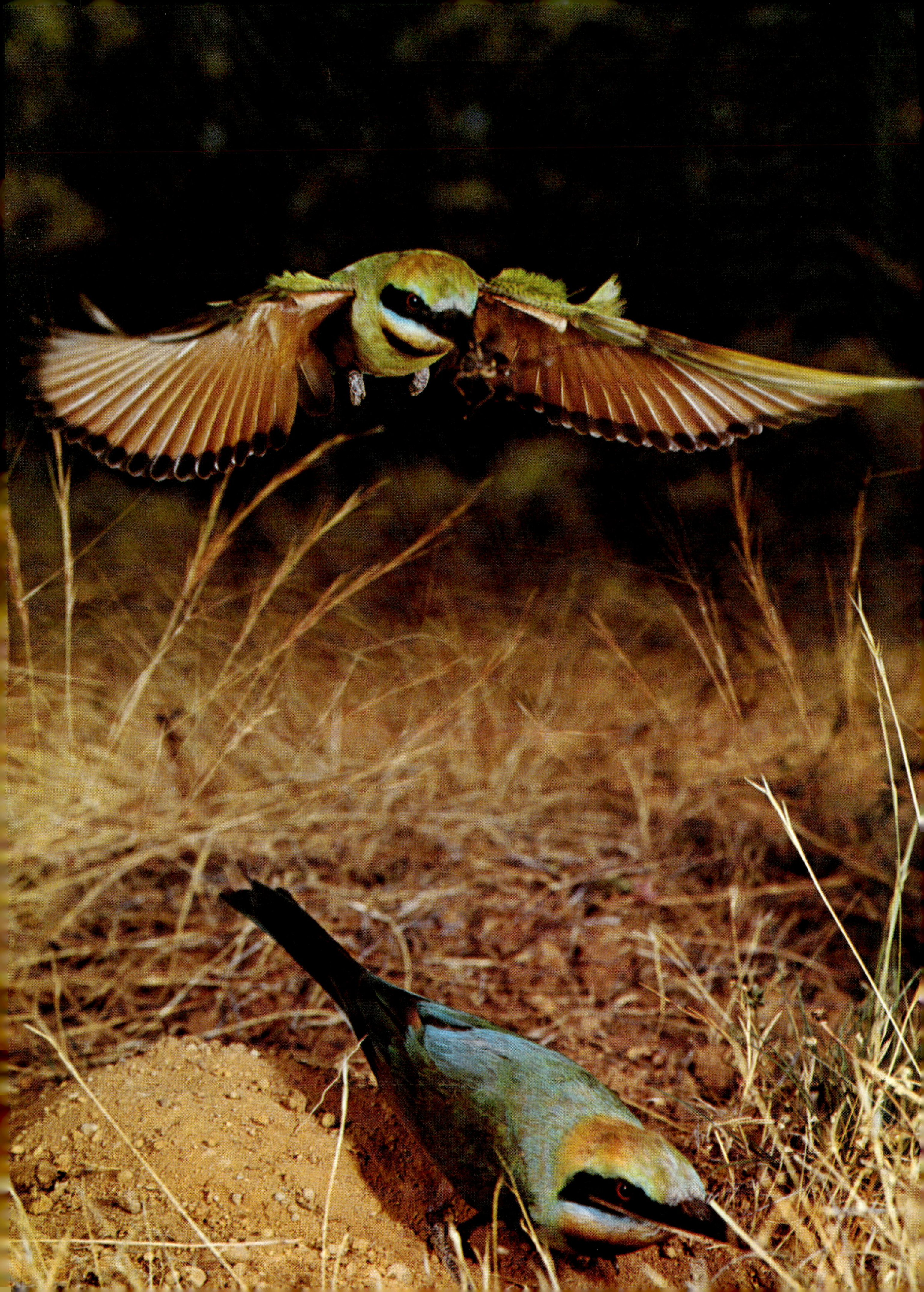

The Fairy Martin has a nest tunnel usually below ground level — but it builds rather than digs, each chamber and entrance spout requiring a thousand or more small mud pellets, and embedded among hundreds of others in a colony in a shallow cave of rock or overhanging river bank. Except for this brief contact with the ground for nesting, this martin, Hylochelidon ariel, *is a bird of the open air, hawking for insects high overhead, or skimming the water surface, and is found widely distributed across the continent.*

temperatures on cold, windy or wet days of early spring.

Close examination of the tiny tunnel of the pardalote reveals a number of fascinating features always present. The tunnel entrance is small, barely one inch across, and well hidden. Any intruder looking into the tunnel sees what is apparently a "dead end" about twelve inches in from the entrance. It may appear that a root has obstructed the way, forcing the digger to abandon his effort at this spot, for the tunnel may be seen to terminate at a solid wall of bark. But that is the nest, its entrance cunningly constructed above the general level of the tunnel roof, so that the incubating diamond bird can peer out, and see down the tunnel to the outside world, but from the outside cannot be seen when settled into its nest.

The secure subterranean nest may confer other advantages. For example, builders of open, cup-shaped nests and even those occupying domed nests, must remain on the eggs or small young for most of the day in chilly weather. But even in cold wet weather the pardalotes appear to be able to spend a far greater proportion of their time off the nest than could the owners of nests exposed to the elements in tree or shrub. Subterranean temperature tends to be more constant than the prevailing air temperature — cooler in summer, warmer in winter, which must benefit both the

Symmetrical markings from which the Spotted Pardalote derives its common name — and its scientific description, Pardalotus punctatus — *show clearly as the male dives into the entrance of his nest tunnel. Taken from above, this picture captures the moment as his wings fold before he plummets into the narrow opening.*

early nesting pardalotes and the summer nesting rainbow birds.

Though common in coastal forests, leaf-sized diamond birds are hard to see in the crowns of tall trees. Only at nesting time do they come to ground to give an admiring observer a glimpse of the jewel-like pattern of rich colours. After nesting time small family parties may be encountered. Moving through the foliage in constant search of tiny insects on leaves and flowers, the birds can be followed by the frequent click of beaks, and by the soft calls, repeated again and again to the point of monotony.

Contrasting with the inconspicuous habits of the tiny diamond birds are those vociferous aerial acrobats, the bee-eaters, whose high-pitched calls break the hush of the midday heat. Over paddocks and forest clearings the orange wings flash against blue sky as bee-eaters glide, twist and turn in pursuit of fast-flying insects, though all other birds are silent and hidden in shady foliage.

Shown twice life size, young pardalotes stretch long scraggy necks for tiny, pollen-dusted insects gathered from flowering wattles and eucalypts of the forest above.

The Bee-eater, Rainbow Bird, Gold-digger, Berrin Berrin or *Merops ornatus* of science, is variously named for the bees in its insect fare, for its beauty of plumage, for the tunnel it drills for a nest, and long ago, by the Aborigines, whose "Berrin Berrin" expresses as well as any words, the rapid notes of the high-pitched calls.

These bee-eaters migrate from the tropics to take advantage of the abundance of insect life of the southern Australian summer, for they feed exclusively upon large insects caught in flight. The bee-eaters nest late in the year, with the young just hatching when midsummer shade temperatures approach the century. A subterranean nest provides a measure of humid warmth far less damaging than the scorching dry heat of midsummer days.

Other birds nest beneath the ground. Several parrots dig into the mounds of tropical termites, also some kingfishers, while the White-backed and other swallows drill tunnels in sandy soil embankments. The Fairy Martin does not drill, but constructs a nest beneath an overhanging river bank or shallow rocky cave. A thousand small pellets of mud — every one a separate journey from river to nest — adhere to the rocks to form the nest bowl and its long entrance spout.

In favoured spots, these birds build in colonies. The Martins skim the river surface or hawk high over head for tiny insects, dashing straight into the tunnel, so that a large colony presents a picture of constant activity as the swift birds dash in and out of the clustered nests.

When almost ready to leave the nest, the boldest of four young pardalotes intercepted the food supply at the tunnel entrance, with the others close behind.

These pardalotes, also called diamond birds, invariably drill their little tunnel near the top of a bank of soil, perhaps to avoid waterlogging, for they begin to nest near the end of winter. The female is in the tunnel entrance, the brighter male has just landed on the twigs below. Both share all tasks of digging, nest construction, incubation, and feeding of the young.

Crouched in a tiny tunnel barely an inch and a half high, the male Spotted Pardalote feeds the young in their subterranean nest, where they are hidden from the outside world, for pardalotes cunningly construct the opening into this nest slightly above the level of the tunnel ceiling, and out of the line of sight from the tunnel entrance.

MISTLETOES

Scattered throughout Australia from coastal forests to the driest parts of the interior still capable of supporting plant life, are some sixty species of mistletoe, parasitic on trees, shrubs and even grasses.

Some steal the nutrient sap containing the food manufactured in the leaves of the host. Others tap a tree's supply of water and dissolved minerals, as it rises through woody vessels of trunk and branch and divert the flow to their own thick leaves which, like the leaves of any normal plant, are able to convert the inorganic minerals and water (by using the energy of sunlight) into the organic substances of the mistletoe plant body.

There are mistletoes of branch, trunk, and root. Of tropical forest and of the mulga. There are some entirely dependent upon a host — three of which have completely lost their own root structure and have developed instead the penetrating haustorium. Others like Nuytsia, the western Christmas Tree, have their own roots, but tap the roots of others as a supplementary food supply.

Perhaps more than a little of the success of the aerial mistletoe is due to a small scarlet-and-black bird, *Dicaeum*, the Mistletoe Bird. Swallow-like in size and shape and flight, but with irridescent metallic blue-black, crimson and white plumage, this small bird has with the mistletoe a truly symbiotic relationship.

A male Mistletoe Bird with beak full of sticky mistletoe seeds. At his feet hang green berries of the mistletoe. The bird skilfully nips the centre of a ripe yellow berry, pulls away the thin skin, and takes the seed which is thickly covered in a sweet but very sticky white layer: the food of the mistletoe bird.

In a clump of mistletoe on the branch of a gum, the mistletoe bird collects seeds for its young in a nearby nest. Above his head hangs an empty skin, cleanly cut by a beak which appears to be shaped for the purpose.

In nature's world of wonders, adaptation of plant to bird, and bird to plant is another example of the vital relationship between all living things in the biotic community. The development in *Loranthus* of sticky berries attractive to birds, is easily understandable. The development in the nervous system of the mistletoe bird of a reflex action causing this constant side to side movement, ensuring that the voided seed will lodge on the twig, where it germinates and grows, is a greater wonder of evolution.

Much mention has been made of the family *Loranthus*, which in Australia comprises many species of mistletoe plants parasitic not only on the branches of gums and wattles, but also on the roots of trees, shrubs and even grass. *Nuytsia floribunda*, of trees, shrubs and even grass. Nuytsia floribunda, the golden Christmas Tree, is a root parasite, and of the *Loranthus* family. It is believed to represent the primitive form; a position indicated by primi-tive floral structure and by parasitic attachment to roots rather than to aerial branches. The most specialized forms of the family *Loranthus* are aerial parasites, and it is believed that the adoption of aerial growth may have evolved from a direct transfer — from terrestrial to epiphytic growth — following the lodging and germination of seeds (carried perhaps by birds) on the branches of a host tree. The mistletoe roots, running along branches as they would underground to seek host roots, made their connection instead in the branches. Humid tropical rain forest would offer a most likely situation for this, so it is notable that Malaysia is considered the centre of origin of the *Loranthideae*.

The Christmas tree *Nuytsia*, which displays its wealth of gold through summer months, is the sole representative of its genus and is unique to sandy western coastal plains. There is nothing in the appearance of this tree to suggest its parasitic habits. The leaves appear quite capable of food production, while the roots appear capable of supplying its mineral and water requirements. For a time the exact nature of its parasitic habit was in doubt until the discovery of long underground stems, of a very brittle nature, which run outwards from the tree for great distances. At intervals the stems give off upright shoots which emerge as suckers, and also thin, soft roots which spread until the root of another plant is encountered. The *Nuytsia* root then rings the host root with a collar-like haustorium. Through this it diverts for its own use the food-laden sap flowing from the leaves of the host plant down to feed the roots. The main object of the Christmas tree's parasitic habit appears to be the supplementary food supply which includes nitrogenous substances. The root attachment seems most important to young plants.

Seedling Christmas trees seem rare in nature, but the suckers from underground stems common, particularly after a fire. These suckers may easily be distinguished from seedlings. The former emerge from the ground as thick stems with few scattered leaves, for the food supply comes from the parent tree. Growth is rapid for the same reason, and a sucker may grow four feet in a year. The seedling, however, is quite independent, and so is more amply supplied with leaves in which to synthesize its own food. Growth of the seedling is very slow, and it must find host roots, even if only of grasses.

For the bird, the advantages of the diet of sticky-sweet mistletoe berries are twofold. One advantage must be that this is an exclusive niche: a food source relatively free from serious competition from other birds. Some honeyeaters and others do share the fruit of the mistletoe, but only *Dicaeum* is really specialized, even to the extent of a digestive tract which by-passes the stomach to give the seeds the shortest passage through the intestine; for each hard seed has only a thin, viscid coat of useful food

Many seeds must be consumed in the shortest time to maintain the fuel so rapidly burned by such an active creature. Most birds, and the small active species in particular, with their high body temperature, have a particularly high metabolic rate, and must eat almost constantly to maintain life at such a level.

A second great advantage conferred by this specialization on mistletoe berry seed lies in its universal availability. Examination of the distribution of the mistletoe bird shows a range covering most parts of the Australian mainland, from southern forests to the tropical north and through the centre wherever there are trees and scrub. *Dicaeum* is a nomad ranging far and wide to follow the fruiting mistletoe; it is found throughout the full range of forest types of the Australian continent. All are home to the mistletoe bird, because in all forests, whether of great gums, or dwarfed

A clump of flowering mistletoe, Loranthus Miquellii, *hanging from the branches of a wandoo shows long pendulous leaves often of attractive ochre and coppery colours. The mistletoe has no roots, but taps the water and mineral supply rising in the tree by a penetrating and absorbing growth known botanically as the* haustorium. *The mistletoe leaves have chlorophyll, so it makes its own food from water and minerals taken from the host, using captured sunlight energy.*

LEFT:

To a nest suspended from treetop twigs the male of the species brings mistletoe seeds. Wings are half closed; his speed carries him upwards. The nest is outstanding. Constructed of soft fibres, the greyish-white cocoons of case moths, and spiders' egg sacs and webs, it is of strong and of felt-like consistency, neat and colourful, and decorated on top with the brown castings of wood-boring caterpillars. A nest once collected in central Australia was found to weigh, including the portion of twig to which it was attached, only seven grains. The three eggs are pure white.

OPPOSITE:

Bluff Knoll, highest peak of the Stirling Range, rises behind the sunlit gold of a Christmas Tree, Nuytsia, *flowering in the foothills. The range is a national park, sanctuary for wildlife, and for many wildflowers found only on the cool, moist peaks. The Christmas Tree is a member of the mistletoe family, but attaches to the roots instead of the branches of other trees.*

A close view of the male mistletoe bird at the nest shows the metallic blue sheen on his black plumage. Colour in the animal world is of two types: those due simply to pigments, and others due to the structural nature of the surface. Pigment colours, which always include red, black and brown, remain unaltered under changing lighting direction, for these colours are due to coloured substances in the material of the feathers. Blue, violet and green are structural colours — light rays are scattered by feather barbules and airspaces, these short wavelengths being strongly reflected. As this bird moves a glint of iridescent blue, coming not from fixed pigment, but from glancing beams of light, glides across the surface of his black-pigmented plumage.

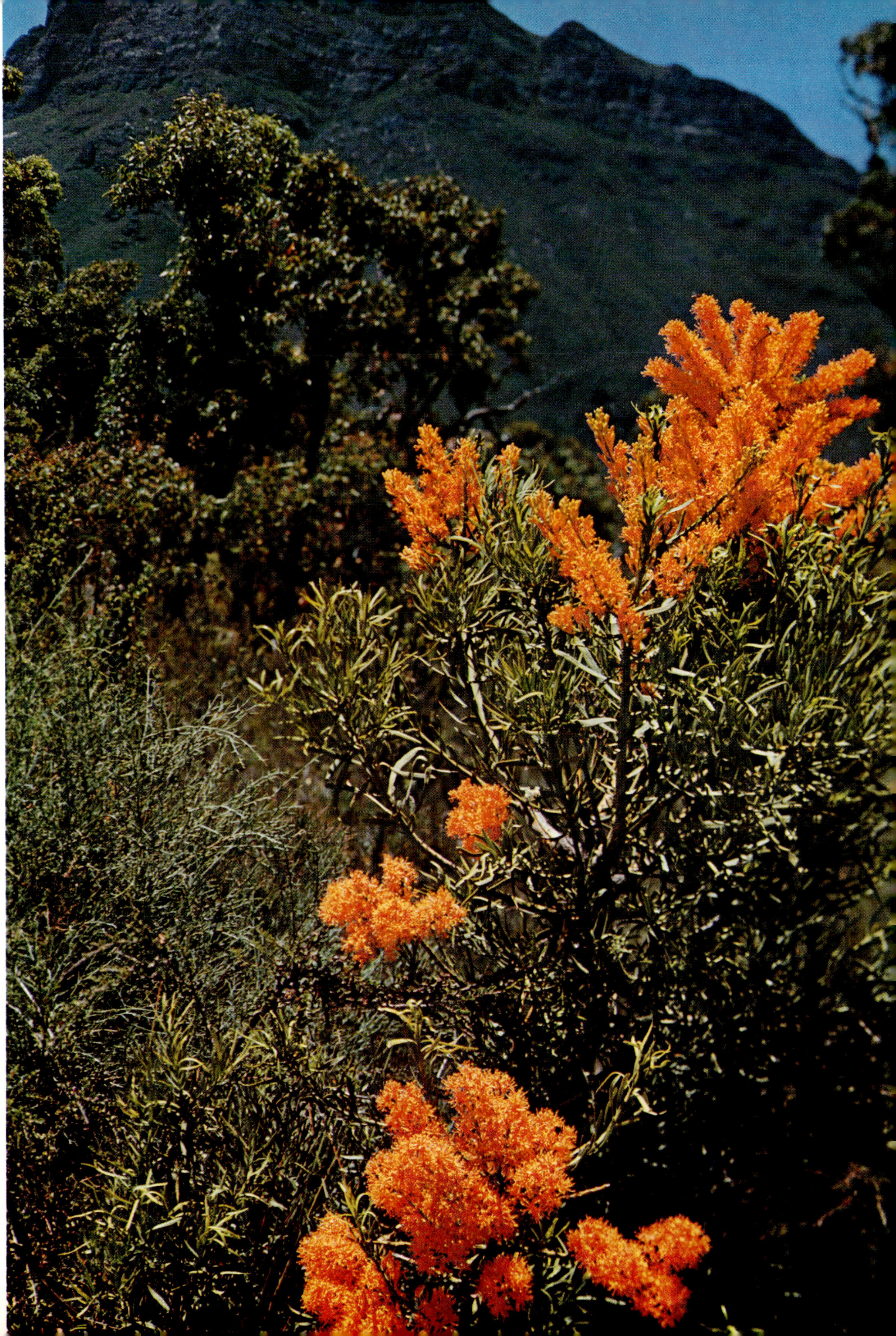

The grey and white female Dicaeum *takes away mistletoe seeds now with little left of the original nutritive coat. The viability of the seeds remains unimpaired in passage through the birds. Wiped or dropped on any suitable twig they quickly germinate, penetrate, and grow. These birds are considered the chief disseminator of the mistletoe.*

mallee or mulga scrub, there are some species of mistletoe and always some with ripe berries. But this is only half the story. If the relationship between *Dicaeum* and the mistletoes is symbiotic, then it must be advantageous to the plant, as well as for the bird, and a study of the habits of the bird shows that the mistletoe bird does assist these plants.

The mistletoes — all members of the family *Loranthus*, are parasites. Rather than send down roots for soil minerals and water, they attach to the branches of trees, and form connections to tap their hosts' supply of water and dissolved minerals passing upwards from roots to leaves. Diverted to the mistletoes' leaves these materials are converted to food as in any normal green plant.

But to spread from tree to tree, *Loranthus* requires a disseminator — a bird or animal which will unwittingly take seeds to a new host tree. To this end the seeds are sweet and sticky when ripe, and food for a variety of birds, particularly *Dicaeum*. There are two possible ways by which the mistletoe bird could carry the sticky seeds from one host tree to another. One presumes that the seeds (which are extremely sticky when removed from the yellow enclosing skin) will occasionally stick to the outside of a mistletoe bird's beak so that it will wipe its beak on a thin twig, where the seed will adhere, germinate, penetrate, and grow.

But *Dicaeum* is extremely adept at handling these sticky seeds. When ripe, mistletoe seeds hang within a yellow skin. The mistletoe bird snips this jacket centrally, dropping the lower half, and extracting the sticky berry (photo). Somehow the bird can do this when already holding in its beak not one, but two berries already collected. It seems unlikely that any bird so skilled in this essential procedure would often be forced to wipe — and waste — berries on branches because it could not manage them! Close observation does show that *Dicaeum* often wipes his beak on a twig especially often feeding young in the nest — but only to wipe away the sticky residue.

The alternative hypothesis suggests that the *Loranthus* seed sticks to a branch, where it has fallen after passing through the mistletoe bird. Tests have shown that such seeds germinate as well as any, for the bird digests only the glutinous outer layer, leaving the viability of the seed unimpaired, and its outside still very sticky. But it would seem that the chance of any seeds voided by *Dicaeum* falling upon a suitable lower branch and adhering, is slight; and so it would be, but for some trend of evolution which has imparted to the mistletoe bird a peculiar twisting habit. When perched, the restless bird seems never to keep still. It constantly turns this way and that, so that its body is as often along the twig as across it. This behaviour makes the frequent lodgement of sticky mistletoe seeds on suitable thin twigs a certainty, and establishes *Dicaeum* as the chief disseminator of the mistletoe.

FOREST LIFE

WOODLANDS EAST and west, provide sanctuary for a wealth of wildlife: bright birds at all levels and leaf canopy to branches and bracken; marsupial carnivore "cats", a tiger-striped *Thylacine* "wolf", and a cunning hunter-scavenger, the pouched Tasmanian Devil. Herbivores from Potoroo and Pademelon to the Pretty-face Wallaby and Great Grey Kangaroo; nocturnal phalangers with ringed tails and grasping feet; the volplaners from Greater Glider to diminutive Feathertail — these are but few of the creatures finding food and sanctuary in the sheltering forests from southern bush to Queensland jungle scrub.

Every creature of the forest has a niche: each has evolved with tree and shrub, with the sun, soil and rains that have formed the character of any patch of bushland.

All fit a mosaic; an ecosystem in which each has place and way of life that mould size and shape, colour and habit.

Most finches are birds of open grassland plains, but the Red-eared Firetail, *Zonæginthus oculatus*, is a denizen of forest undergrowth where its solitary habits — except only after nesting, when it may be seen in small family parties — contrast with the gregarious flocking of the finches of wide northern plains.

Though one of the most primitive of the many Australian grass-finches, this large and particularly attractive firetail is most efficiently adapted to the

Rearing back on their tails, Great Grey Kangaroos grapple and kick with long-clawed feet; these deadly claws have taken the lives of attacking dogs and men. Having gained a grip with forepaws, an angry or defensive kangaroo can stand up on its tail to disembowel an enemy with one rip of the long claws of the back feet.

The Great Grey, or Forester Kangaroo, Macropus major, is an inhabitant of coastal forests, where continued slaughter poses a much greater threat to the survival of this kangaroo and certain rare wallabies, than to the hardy Red Kangaroo and Euro of inland scrub and the north.

A flying male brings insects for ever-hungry young. Golden whistlers are inhabitants of forests on eastern and western coasts, extended from Tasmania to New Guinea and islands of the Solomon group, this bird has more variants, or subspecies, than any other. Some island forms now have little colour. The song of the golden male is one of the commonest forest sounds in spring, when it pours forth powerfully as he sings to protect his territory — his nest and an acre or two of the bush.

OPPOSITE:

Golden Wattle: Acacia. *More than any other this is the flower that is Australia. Though the west with more than 350 species has more than half the world's acacias, this tree is from Australia's eastern coast.* Acacia podalyriifolia, *the Queensland Silver Wattle, carries glaucous pods and leaves giving a powdered or silvered effect to the foliage, which disappears beneath golden flowers in the winter months.*

The behaviour of a bird is controlled by instinct to a great extent. The events of its life are for the most part met with inherited patterns of behaviour. Each bird builds the exact form of nest characteristic of its species, without trial and error, or experiment. Each species has its own courtship display actions and other purposeful displays, each a series of actions triggered by some natural stimulus in the bird's surroundings. Care of the young follows this pattern of set action and reaction: the hatching brings a stimulus, the bright, gaping mouths of the young triggering in the parents a desire to give food.

This female of the Golden Whistler, Pachycephala pectoralis, *has none of the bright colour of her mate above. Other whistler species may be less colourful, but one, the Rufous Whistler, is renowned for its rich and varied song, which far surpasses the attractive calls of this golden species.*

78

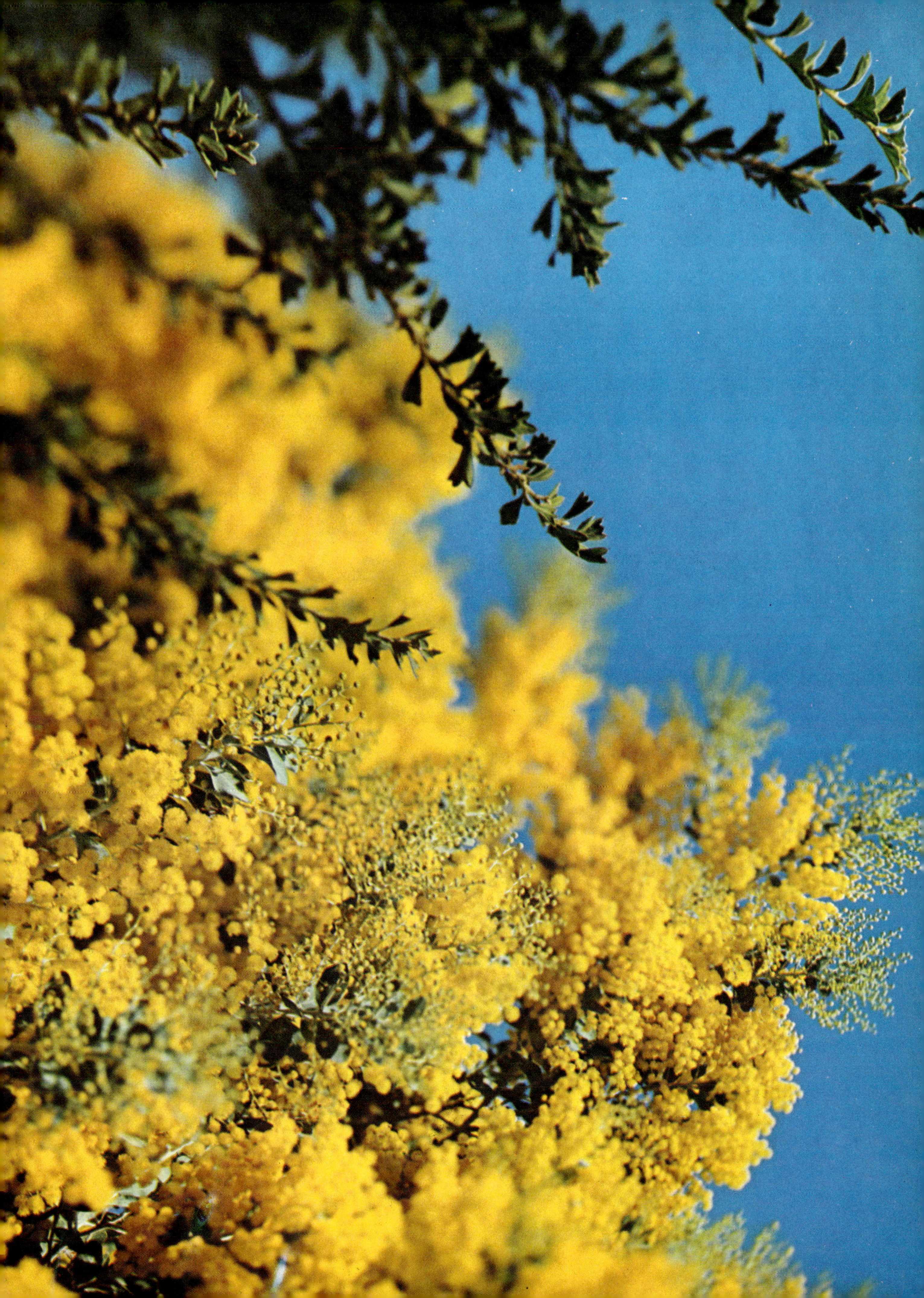

dense environment of a forest habitat. Its flight straight and low, with deviations only to weave among trees or through the undergrowth, whereas the finches of the wide inland plains swarm from the grass with the chattered flight calls that keep the birds together throughout the flock's erratic flight. The forest-dwelling finch has no flocking call. It is silent in flight but has other calls more useful within the closer confines of its habitat: a low, wavering "identity call" by which a pair maintains contact when foraging, and softer sounds uttered at the nest.

In timbered country the Red-eared Firetail nests at exceptional heights, but inhabits also a region of south-coastal scrub where such high sites are not available. A long and bulky nest is hidden in the crown of a tall sapling, or in masses of hanging foliage. An enclosed chamber and a long horizontal entrance tunnel are laced and wrapped with long stems of green grass and of fringe-flowered *Thysanotus* creepers. A lining of feathers completes the inner chamber of a nest which ornithologists consider to represent the evolutionary peak of nestbuilding among Australian finches.

Both sexes share the tasks of construction, incubation, and the feeding of four, five or six young firetails. In their enclosed fortress the inner chamber is completely concealed, so that on arrival at the nest's long entrance tunnel, a bird returning from an hour or two of foraging will exchange with its hidden mate soft, intimate calls: an enquiry and answer by which it can discover whether conditions within are normal and safe. This behaviour differs greatly from that of the Zebra and other grassland finches which dash from their smaller, more open nests immediately the relieving mate lands nearby.

Roosting nests also are built. These are nearer the favoured feeding places, often in lower scrub, and of exposed situation; rough, unlined, and with little of the long entrance tunnel that is seen on the breeding nests.

Native grasses scattered through open scrub patches constitute the feeding niche of this rare finch of south-western forests. Perched on fallen branch or stem it reaches out with either foot to bend down the grass heads and take the seeds. Throughout the year firetails forage within a territory extending a hundred yards or more around the nest site, but territorial defence against others of the species is limited to the immediate vicinity of the nest, and at times several nests may be built in close proximity where slender saplings offer the most suitable sites.

Most birds hold territories which they may defend by song, threat or battle against others of their species, the area of their bushland claim depending upon food requirements and the resources of their region. These territories serve to disperse and control the avian population of the forest or other habitat, though some reduce their defended territory almost to the nest itself. Of these the sea birds are the greatest colonial nesters, clustering in thousands on island breeding grounds. Some birds form smaller colonies. Fairy Martins (also a species dependent on a mobile food supply, the airborne insects) cluster their bottle-shaped nests of mud under an overhanging rock or river bank.

Such group nesting is least common among forest birds, which tend to disperse through the favoured zones; heavy timber or open woodland, hillside scrub or dense, damp thickets. However there are some exceptions where groups of birds rather than pairs hold territory. Western Magpies, *Gymnorhina dorsalis*, have been shown to form strongly-territorial groups numbering up to twenty birds which vigorously defend an area averaging perhaps a hundred acres. The males, plumaged in sharply-contrasting black and white, are more or less promiscuous within the group, and give only minor assistance in feeding the young ones, though always quick to rally with diving attacks on any possible predator.

The Splendid Wrens of woodland undergrowth, and Red-winged Wrens of the dense damp thickets hunt and nest in family parties. Their groups number up to four or five individuals, with territorial reaction, display and active defence characteristic not only of the dominant male but also of mature but non-breeding males of the group.

On his own territory a bird is almost invincible, and the wren is no exception. The presence of an "outsider" triggers challenging song, threat posture and finally physical attack with beak and claw. Usually an intruding male wren behaves as if feeling the guilt of trespass when met by an indignant owner of the territory. Retreating after brief song battle he takes the shortest route home, flying silently and with blue-black feathers fluffed out as a sign of appeasement to the victor.

Unlike most bush creatures, the Numbat, Myrmecobius fasciatus, is abroad in daylight hours, feeding on termites which are exposed by scratching aside small fallen logs or digging among twig and leaf litter. It is found in open, dry wandoo forest in south-western Australia where hollow logs are its refuge, and formerly in the Murray River area, where it is probably now extinct.

As distinctive in behaviour as in form, is the Lyrebird, famed for its spectacular displays in which filamentous plumes arch far to the front in a lacy, shimmering screen; it also has a powerful song, and is a skilful mimic.

Each male constructs display mounds. As many as fourteen may be scattered through a territory of four or five acres of south-eastern schlerophyll forest, where the Mountain Ash canopy covers a tangled understorey of acacias, tree-ferns and bracken in a dense, damp habitat.

The male Lyrebird is polygamous, competing in display for acceptance by any female attracted to the mound by his song and dance performance. She alone builds the nest and raises a single young. More commonly, pairs hold territory. In spring the male sings a challenge from favoured perches around the chosen site, but here and there may be forced to retreat as others of his kind stake out adjoining claims.

Golden Whistlers (and the Rufous Whistler of open woodlands) possess powerful, rich territorial calls and song. The song of the golden male is one of the commonest sounds in spring when it pours forth from trees bordering his territory of an acre or two of coastal forest. The sound of these ringing calls may attract a mate, but, more important, she recognizes him as a male of property, able to hold foraging space for a family. At times a duet of softer calls between male and female keeps contact through dense forest thickets, and strengthen the bond between the pair.

Almost as though rich song makes colourful plumage redundant, it is frequently the plain bird that is the renowned songster. Among whistlers, the richest song and most attractive and varied repertoir of notes belong to the Rufous Whistler, *Pachycephala rufiventris*. Similar in plumage pattern to the Golden Whistler, a Rufous is pale brown where the former is bright yellow.

More inclined to solitary life than the birds, are the nocturnal marsupials of the Australian bush. The Tiger Cat, *Dasyurops maculatus*, is a powerful, stubborn and well-equipped arboreal carnivore whose clawed feet bear serrated pads which mark it as a treetop hunter. Like the smaller, more terrestrial native cats, *Dasyurinus*, it is an uncommon inhabitant of mainland forests, remaining plentiful only in rugged Tasmanian bushland. These carnivores are marsupial, quite unrelated to the feline cats of other lands, but comparable in teeth and claws and hunting skills.

Not yet rare in the wild scrub of Tasmania is the Tasmanian Devil, *Sarcophilus harrisi*, of black and bulky body, stiff-necked and crudely shaped. A powerful predator and scavenger and a solitary nocturnal hunter able to take a wallaby or tackle a tiger snake, the Devil is more often present than seen, hiding by day among rocks, holes and hollow logs. But though the marsupial killers, large and small, are of solitary habits, other animals are more often of friendly disposition and commonly associate with their fellows.

Sugar Gliders, *Petaurus breviceps*, venture from hollow limbs of daytime retreats in small family groups, to soar from branch to trunk in glides of up to fifty yards, feeding on insects, buds, and blossom of gum and shrub. Also gregarious is the mouse-sized *Acrobates*, Pygmy or Feathertail Glider. In family parties it hunts insects and nectar, retreating to a nest of leaves or bark hidden in broken branch or knothole. In gliding flight the feather-like tail serves as a rudder. Though common in eastern coastal and mountain forests, the diminutive, nocturnal Feathertail is not often seen.

The Yellow Robin (shown here at a nest camouflaged with hanging strips of bark) shows evidence of the part played by the slowly changing climatic cycles of a continent in the evolution of new species. This Western Yellow Robin, Eopsaltria griseogularis *is very similar to the yellow robins of the east, but differs in having between the yellow breast and white throat, a grey band.*

At one time the eastern form extended in unbroken distribution to the west coast, but the expanding desert in a long dry cycle has for centuries isolated the smaller population in the south-west corner. Now showing small differences (the grey band) as genetic mutations adapt them to the western environment, the western robins are classified as a separate species, but are considered by some authorities not to have reached that status, and to be no more than a variety of the eastern bird.

OPPOSITE:

In winter and early spring the male Superb Lyrebird, Menura novae-hollandiæ, *exhibits in spectacular display his plumes and voice, trying to attract to the mound a female of his species. At the peak of the dance these long plumes will be thrown forward enveloping him and his mate in a patterned veil.*

In the nest cells of a paper wasp, Polistes, *colony the larval wasps hang head downward, and are attended by the worker wasps. But these adults are motivated by no tender maternal instinct — they bring food because the larvae give automatically in return a drop of some much-relished liquid. This phenomenon of mutual feeding probably keeps the daughter wasps attached to their home colony. With winter the colony dies away, only young fecundated queens surviving to start new colonies in the spring.*

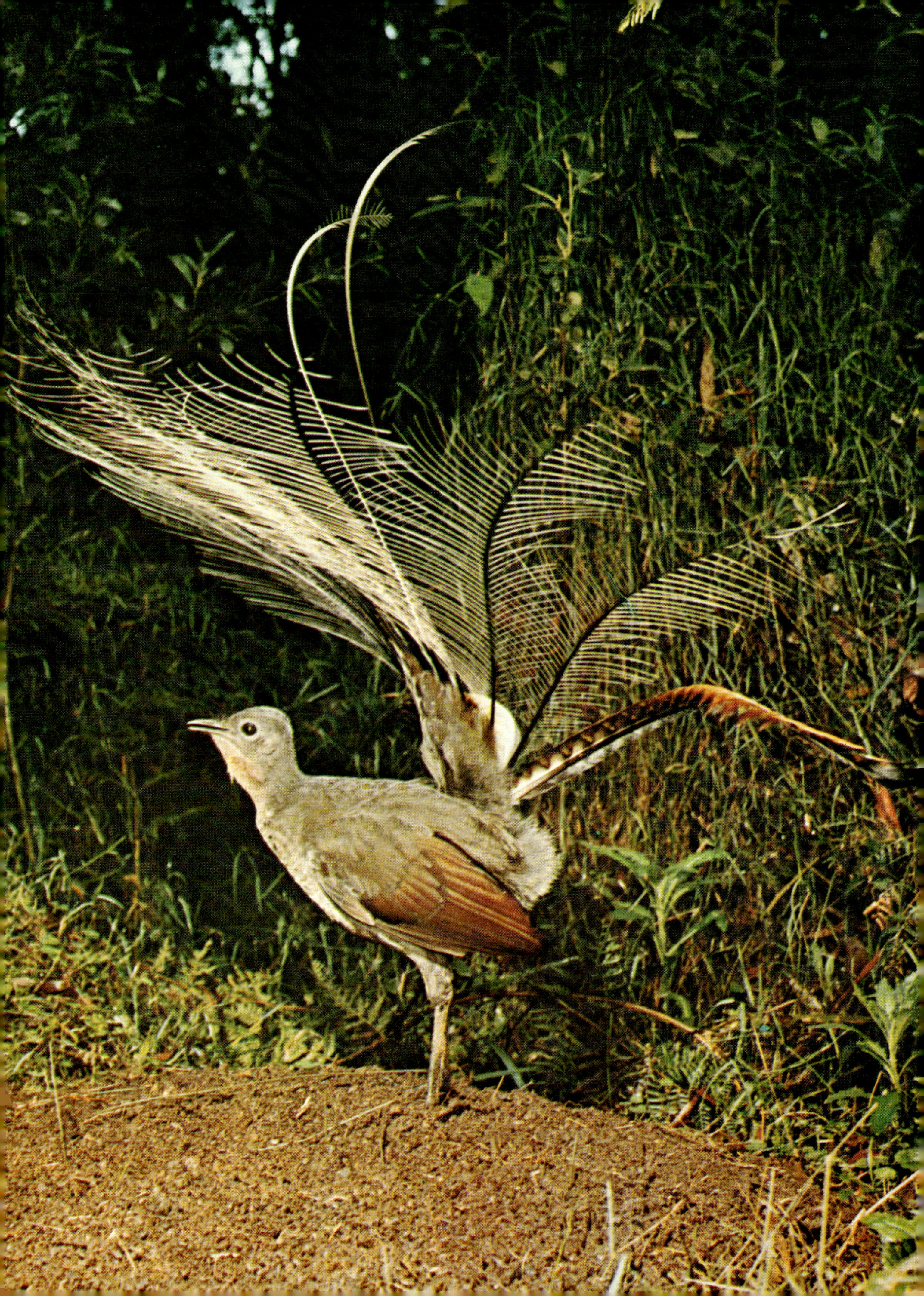

Grazers of the open plains gather together; in the mob there is a greater chance of survival. The Great Grey, or Forester, *Macropus major*, like other kangaroos is gregarious, gathering at dusk in mobs to feed in forest clearings. There is neither leader nor sentinel. Any kangaroo alarmed will thump its tail and leap for cover, scattering the mob in panic, each animal bounding at random towards the sheltering scrub.

As forest companions of the Great Grey are many wallabies, among them some of the most attractive in the bush: the Red-legged Pademelon, the Pretty-face or Whip-tail, the Swamp Wallaby, and woodland forms of the Wallaroo in the east; the Black-gloved and Tammar or Dama wallabies in the west.

The ancestors of these unique and graceful creatures are thought to have been treetop dwellers. Off shoots of the phalanger stock first appeared in terrestrial form as small, rat-like creatures with characteristics between those of possum, bandicoot and kangaroo.

At the time of their arrival in Australia, perhaps via some connecting land link, marsupials represented the most successful mammalian plan. The first placentals may then have existed, but as an almost insignificant minority still experimenting with all the advantages bestowed by the faster growth of a full-term embryo, as compared to the slow final growth made in the pouch of the marsupial.

Later, placentals became dominant but did not reach the isolated Australian continent until comparatively recent times, perhaps 25 million years ago, when the first rodents may have arrived clinging to driftwood, and bats by flight. Much

At the peak of the dance the long plumes are thrown forward, often completely hiding the lyrebird's head. There are only two species of lyrebird — this, the Superb, and the less spectacular Albert Lyrebird. The females nest and raise the young unaided by the male. Among the accomplishments of the Superb Lyrebird is its outstanding mimicry of forest sounds, particularly the calls of other birds.

The Kookaburra, a giant kingfisher, preys largely upon reptiles and rodents, but also takes small birds, and in this respect is less welcome in areas where it does not occur naturally — it has been introduced into Western Australia and Tasmania.

later came Aboriginal man, bringing a half-domesticated dog, the Dingo.

Running wild through the mainland the fast and cunning Dingo must have become the dominant predator, displacing and apparently rendering extinct the large but primitive marsupial carnivores, the *Thylacine* and the Marsupial Devil, which today are confined to Tasmania (where the former may recently have become extinct) being recorded only as fossil remains on the mainland.

Now Australia's distinctive wildlife is retreating before an influx of foreign placentals: cats, foxes, rabbits and sheep. But more serious is the loss of habitat as land is cleared, more than a million acres of bushland going beneath the plough each year.

Six of a hundred and thirty-three marsupials are certainly extinct, twenty-eight others have not been seen for years. Most of these were lost years ago with the initial spread of farming and grazing; others continue to cling to any remaining suitable habitat.

The Numbat, a small, striped marsupial anteater, is probably extinct where formerly found in the Murray River district, now existing in parts of south-western wandoo forests, and perhaps in the Everard Range in the northern part of South Australia. In its daylight feeding this anteater is exceptional, for most forest animals are completely nocturnal. With clawed paws it scratches into rotted wood, and with long, extensile, sticky tongue extracts the white-ants cleanly from their galleries. Its vital refuge is the litter of hollow logs and fallen branches characteristic of wandoo

The rare Red-eared Firetail Firetail Finch marks a departure from the normal finch way of life in many respects. As a habitat it has chosen the seclusion of thick forest undergrowth, a contrast to the open plains of the inland and far north. With this different habitat it has acquired new patterns of behaviour. The flight of this firetail, *Zonæginthus oculatus*, is indirect: suited to weaving through thicker bush. It has become a solitary species, never forming large flocks as do most other finches. Pairs (or at the most small family parties after nesting) maintain contact when feeding on the seeds of grasses among undergrowth by low, wavering calls, but the firetail has no flocking call, by which other finches utter in flight to keep the flock together.

The Red-eared Firetail's nest is a foot-long, bulky structure of long grass, placed in the top of a sapling, in dense hanging foliage, or mistletoe clump. For finches these sites are exceptionally high, few being less than twenty feet, and many forty or fifty feet above the ground. The location in upper foliage necessitates a strong construction, for which the small birds collect grass stems and thin vines two or three feet long, which they tow upwards making slow progress, from branch to branch, until the high site is reached.

Both male and female tend the nest. The long entrance spout obscures the interior, and it is customary for a bird arriving at the nest to call softly — enquiring whether all is well inside — and for the sitting bird to give a soft call in response.

Lorikeets pause at the entrance to their nest hollow — these and many other pairs were nesting when gums of the wandoo forest were flowering. Wandering from region to region with the flowering of forests, this lorikeet, Glossopsitta porphyrocephala, may be seen among the spring blossoms of the stunted mallee scrub, or nesting in midsummer when the tall karris begin to show their creamy flowers in the south. Other colourful species inhabit forests of the east and north—these include the Musk, Red-collared, Scaly-breasted, and Rainbow lorikeets.

LEFT:

Purple-crowned Lorikeets are scarcely longer than the leaves through which they clamber to crush the flowers of gums with short, typically parrot-like beaks, totally unlike the delicate long bill of a honeyeater, before licking out the nectar with brush-tipped tongues. Predominantly green, they are splashed with blue and purple, and with crimson underwing, visible only in flight, but which may be glimpsed fleetingly as the tiny parrots dash through the tree-

woodland. With these shelters it has survived the introduction of the fox, but is most vulnerable to the fires of those endeavouring to tidy the bush.

Less archaic than monotreme and marsupial are Australia's birds. Being able to fly, they have maintained more frequent contact with the major continents, developing with a more balanced representation of the major orders. Yet most families have had sufficient isolation to become distinctive, providing a whole host of feathered creatures found nowhere else in the world. Many have adapted in the face of a changing environment: the Galah for one, aided by the clearing of forests and provision of water, and perhaps by an arid trend of inland climate, has extended its range towards the coasts in east and west. Others are less tolerant of man's encroachment. Red-winged Wren, Red-eared Firetail Finch and many others retreat as the natural conditions are changed, and some have become rare to the point of extinction.

The effective conservation of the birds, mammals and wildflowers requires the preservation of the widest possible variety of habitat. Each tract set aside for this purpose must be kept free of encroaching tourist, recreation or other convenient facility, to remain an example of the original balanced ecosystem.

The nest of the Black-capped Sittella, Neositta pileata, *ranks as a masterpiece in camouflage. Though usually built on a high dead branch away from concealing foliage, the nest is extremely difficult to see, being designed to look like a short broken limb, or natural projection growing out from the real branch. The nest is further camouflaged by the addition of matching bark and moss gathered from the tree in which it is built.*

Even the young are of fluffy grey pattern resembling the grey wood which would normally tip a broken limb. The sittellas perfect the disguise by their behaviour: these birds never fly straight to their nest, but on arriving at the tree with a beakful of insects spiral up the trunk and around the branches in their normal pattern of search, stopping every now and then as if taking an insect or spider from the bark. On reaching the nest branch the birds nonchalantly continue their pretended search past the nest, popping the food into the beak of a young when to the observer on the ground below, and probably to any nearby predator, they seem merely to be giving a casual peck at a spot where a small branch has been broken off.

Converging on a hollow spout which is their nest, Rufous Treecreepers, Climacteris rufa, *bring insect food from tree trunk and branch. Treecreepers and sittellas in Australia take the place of the woodpeckers of other lands, probing bark crevices as they spiral up trunk and branch.*

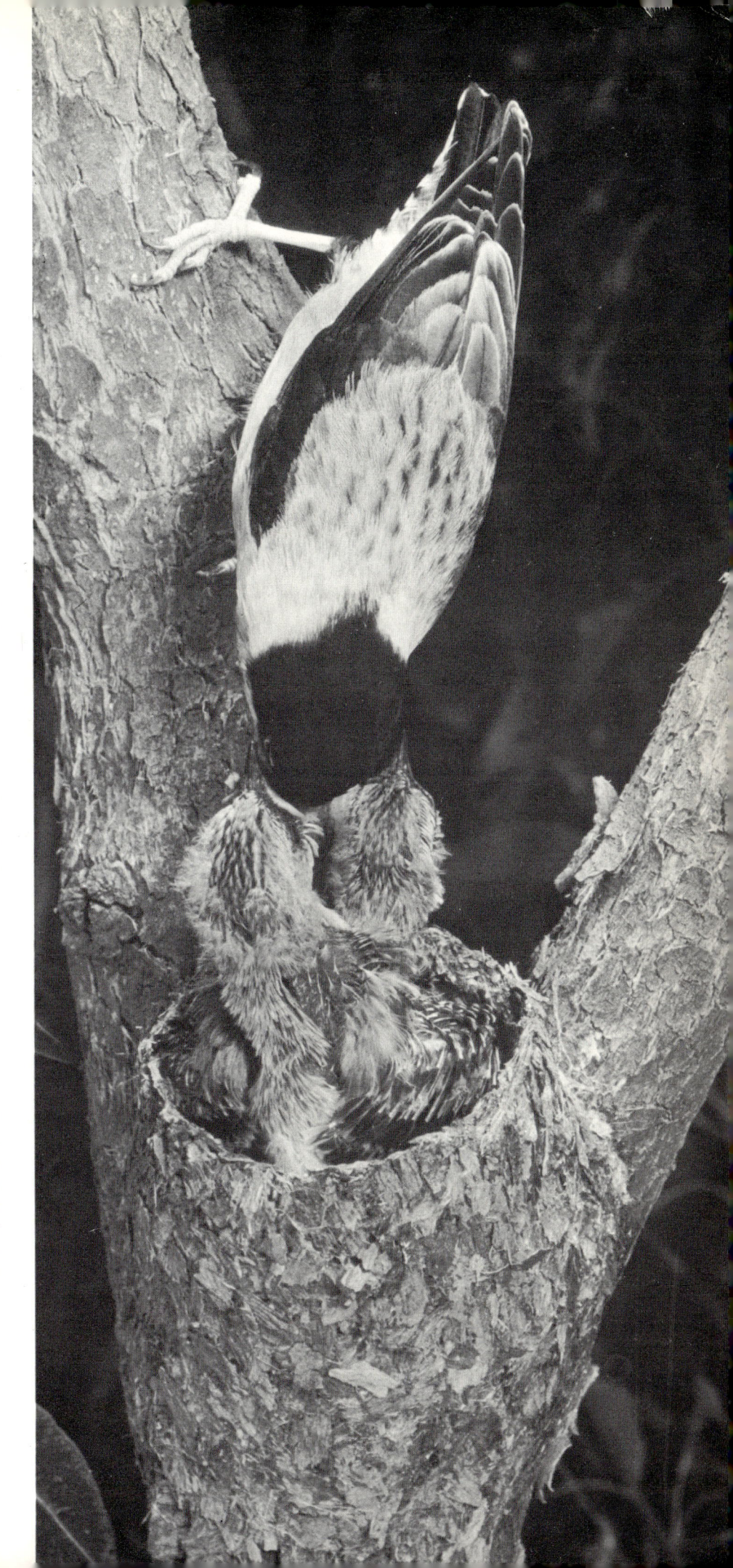

The thirty Calythrix *species range in colour from white to violet, and include red, pink and yellow species. These sand heath plants can easily be recognized by the long, fine points to the calyx lobes, giving a whiskered appearance to the flowers.*

LEFT:
Scarlet fruits of the primitive Macrozamia *lie in a cluster where they have fallen after the bursting of the central cone, a large, pineapple-like structure. The soft red rind surrounding a hard nut is eaten by forest birds and animals, and also by the natives who remove its poisonous qualities by soaking, drying and roasting.*

A small Melaleuca *shrub displays rounded pink heads of flowers: the size of the inflorescences and their prominent, terminal position makes these distinctive among wildflowers.*

THE WESTERN WILDFLOWERS

The wildflowers of Western Australia have become famous not only within that State but far beyond for their unusual structure, exceptional diversity of form, and for richness and variety of colour both in the individual flower and in the massed display.

Many are found only in the west. The south-western flora has developed its distinctiveness in a region long isolated by desert and sea. This land surface is one of the most ancient on earth; plants in the western corner of the continent have had an exceptionally long development undisturbed by major upheavals which elsewhere have formed mountain ranges or broken the ancient lines of plant evolution by complete submergence beneath the sea.

Among plant families most strongly represented in the continent's western sector are acacias in more than three hundred forms; and the myrtles, one of Australia's largest and most important plant families including not only eucalypts (with two hundred and eighteen western species and varieties) but also floral wealth of the groups *Melaleuca*, *Kunzea*, *Verticordia* and *Darwinia*. A third major family of the flora is the *Proteaceae*, or banksia family, which has among its western members the genus *Banksia*, and the often-spectacular trees and shrubs of *Dryandra*, *Grevillea*, *Hakea*, and *Isopogon*.

The exceptional richness of south-western flora is not due to any particularly favourable conditions of soil or climate — on the contrary, many of

Low spreading plants of **Leschenaultia biloba** *cover the forest floor in a carpet of blue. Its colour varies from deep ultramarine on clay soil, to the pure white form growing in the sands of drier regions.*

An inland wattle carries long golden spikes, each a mass of fine fluffy stamens. Australian wattles, or more exactly, acacias, are members of the family Mimosacaceae, *and are legumes, bearing seeds in long pods and flowers in round heads or spikes. Some have feathery, or bipinnate leaves, but many are leafless, the green stems functioning as leaves. Often the thin branchlets are flattened until they look like leaves, but are simple or undivided, whereas the true leaves in this family are always composed of a fern-like pattern of small leaflets.*

the most floriferous and showy forms are confined to sandy and semi-arid fringes of the deserts, where abundance of flower and seed may be a means of survival, ensuring that at least a few seedlings survive the next long drought.

Though most families of western wildflowers are represented also in other parts of Australia, and elsewhere in the world, there are many genera (the biological grouping between family and species) native only to the west, and several instances of small families completely endemic to the region.

One such family contains but a single species, *Cephalotus follicularis*, the Albany Pitcher Plant, with modified leaves shaped as pitchers trapping and digesting insects. Similar in structure and function are the pitchers of the genus *Nepenthes*, of the Malaysian jungles.

A second endemic family is of one genus with two species. The Rainbow Plant, *Byblis gigantea* is one of these, and is notable for the glandular hairs which trap and digest small insects on the stem.

More common than complete families confined to the western wildflower region are the endemic genera. Within the myrtles, family *Myrtaceae*, containing the large and important genus *Eucalyptus*, thirty-three of the eighty genera are found only in Western Australia. One such genus is *Dryandra*, an ancient form with sixty species having stiffly-structured flower heads most commonly of yellow and orange, but including also some metallic bronzed and purple tones.

The widespread family *Amaryllidaceae* contains the bizarre kangaroo-paws, found only in south-western Australia. Though totally different in many respects from flowers anywhere else, the paws have a basic inner similarity of structure which shows their distant relationship to common overseas members of the family, including the "tame" snowdrops and daffodils.

The kangaroo-paws, *Anigosanthos*, appear in bright, sometimes discordant colour schemes: the green flowers and red stems of the Red and Green Paw, *A. manglesii*; yellow, orange, green and maroon on other species. Another, *Macropidia fuliginosa*, is black with green and yellow-tipped flowers. All paws, and others of the family — *Conostylis* and *Blancoa* — are recognizable by woolly, felted stem and flower surfaces.

Other complete genera confined to the west are *Beaufortia*, with sixteen shrub species bearing bright bush flowers of pink, crimson, white and mauve; and the genus *Calothamnus* of twenty-four

Spider orchids, as the Caledenias bearing long leg-like sepals and petals are commonly known, have an ingenious balanced platform, hinged at the base and deeply fringed along the sides. As an insect climbs into the flower on this labellum, it reaches a point of balance, when the "see-saw" platform tips up, so that when this insect comes to depart it must climb backward jammed by its own weight between the tipped labellum and the solid central column, until it has passed the pollen at the anthers. The platform then tips back to its original position, allowing the fly or bee to depart carrying the pollen adhering to its back.

This tipping platform ensures that any insect, as it backs out bearing pollen from a near-by spider orchid will deposit this pollen on the sticky stigma before reaching the anthers, there to take on another pollina which will be carried to the next orchid. Thus the spider orchids avoid self-fertilization, and increase the chances of successful cross-fertilization by which each can draw on the genetic qualities of the orchid population.

The Queen of Sheba is a handsome orchid in crimson, gold and purple, and flowers on the western coastal plains in August. Most orchids have one petal modified to serve an important part in the pollination of the flower, but in this species, Thelymitra variegata, and in others of the Thelymitra (sun orchids) and a few other orchid groups, the labellum is not developed but is retained as a normal petal. In the center of the flowers of orchids is a complex structure known as the column, bearing stigma and anthers. This, with the three sepals, two petals, labellum and ribbed seedbox below the flower, distinguishes all orchids from other flowers.

Bright yellow, streaked with crimson, the Cowslip Orchid, Caladenia flava, is common and widely distributed, and flowers in the spring months from August to October. For its pollination this orchid requires the services of a small native bee which must force its way past a palisade (designed to exclude smaller insects) and under an adhesive pollina to reach the nectar.

Leschenaultia formosa, *a prostrate south-western forest plant, appears from May to October, scattered under trees in red circular patches, often several feet in diameter.*

OPPOSITE:

Isopogons, the cone bushes, bear large heads of rose-pink flowers which are prominent above the stiff foliage. Largest-flowered is Isopogon latifolius, *found only on the peaks of the Stirling Ranges. Shown here is* I. dubius, *native to clay-soil clearings and blackboy flats of the Darling Range.*

The Pink Boronia, Boronia heterophylla, *is a member of a widespread genus of near fifty species including as its most famous member the heavily-scented, brown - and - yellow flowered* B. megastima.

OPPOSITE:

A blue Sun Orchid, Thelymitra, *which like most of Australia's orchids of temperate regions is terrestrial (tropical forms are usually epiphytes). It dies down after flowering, to regenerate annually from underground tubers.*

Though the appearance of this Slipper Orchid is unusual, it is not exceptionally attractive: this orchid's fame is for the astonishing method by which it attracts its insect pollinator, an ichneumon fly. The flower is shaped like a large insect, with thin green petals making long legs. Somehow this flower has developed for the male ichneumon the same mysterious attraction as that which draws him from great distances to the female of his species.

Enamel Orchids are named for the glossy, lacquered surface to the petals. The Pink Enamel, Elythranthera emarginata, *is a low plant of swampy situations.*

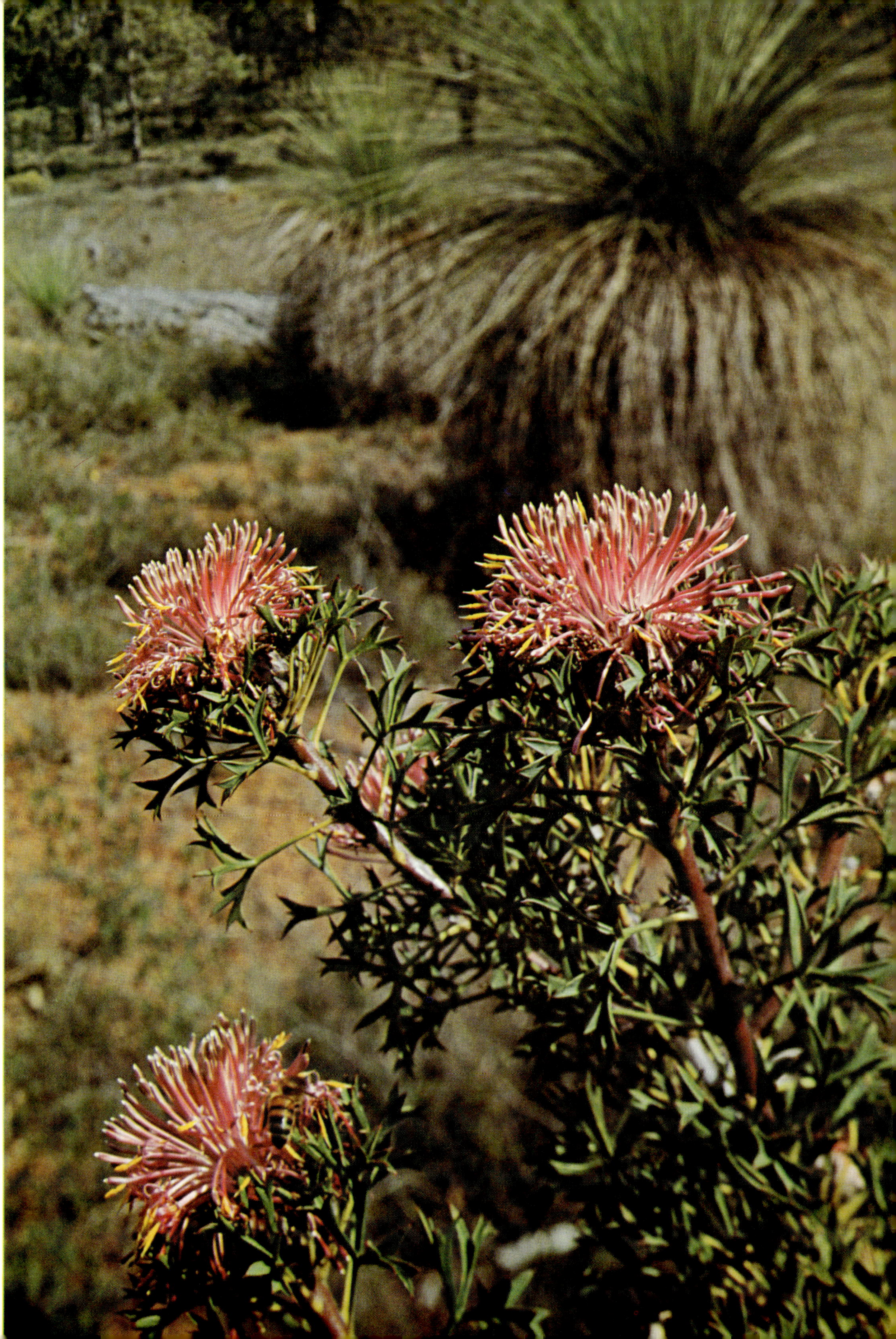

Flowering for more than six months of the year, Grevillea bipinnatifida *grows as a spreading shrub with attractively-divided leaves, and seems always to be bearing at least a few of its pendulous red racemes of hooked flowers. When grown in cultivation, and receiving summer water, it can flower throughout the year. Unlike many Australian plants which retain their seeds for months or years after flowering, the shell-like fruits of grevilleas split and drop their seeds in the season. In the bush the species shows vigorous regrowth and flowering after fire, which usually burns this shrub to the ground.*

species, many of bright colours and popularly known as "one-sided bottlebrushes" when the flowers appear clustered along one side of the stems.

In addition to these families and genera found only in south-western Australia, many large groups are dominantly but not exclusively western, and it is upon these groups that much of the real wealth of this floral region is based. Some, like *Banksia*, have but few outstanding species to the east of the desert divide; others like the eucalypts are strongly representative of all parts of Australia, yet have in the west many of their most outstanding forms.

The lechenaultia family (as the *Goodeniaceae* may commonly be called) contains thirteen genera all with wildflowers in south-western Australia, and of the three hundred flower species, more than two hundred are western. Within this family the genus *Lechenaultia* has twenty south-western species including the famed blue Lechenaultia, *L. Biloba* (a small upright plant giving of its most intense colour on clay soils, and becoming white in northern dry sands) the prostrate scarlet *Lechenaultia formosa,* and others of orange, yellow, violet and green.

Among more than three hundred and fifty native species of *Acacia*, or wattle, Australia's west has tremendous variety. Wattle may be seen at its best in early spring months transforming the hills of the Darling Ranges from green to golden yellow as the massed acacias of the undergrowth, principally *A. pulchella* and *A. drummondii*, burst out in flower. Further inland the big acacia bushes, like the "jam" of wheatbelt farmlands, may vanish beneath a wealth of fluffy yellow flowers. The western wattles range from low undergrowth species of moist south-western forests to the hardy, harsh-foliaged, often-thorny, stunted trees or shrubs which comprise the mulga of arid semi-desert: trees which, despite their normally forbidding appearance and depressing environment, can bear their full share of the floral wealth which in the spring may carpet these inland regions.

The great family *Proteaceae*, though with many species scattered through other parts of Australia and to other continents, reaches a peak of floral beauty in its south-western banksias, which for sheer size of flower spike, for patterned colour, and for intricate detail have no equal.

Apart from *Dryandra*, already mentioned as being a complete genus confined to Western Australia, the banksia family includes also as exceptional, though not exclusively western forms the grevilleas with their long racemes of bright flowers prominently displayed; such species as the White-plumed Grevillea, *G. Leucopteris,* of the sand heath country, and the tall Flame Grevillea, *Grevillea excelsior.*

But western wildflowers are not famed for number and variety alone. Unusual floral structures set the best of Australian plants apart from those of other lands. Few of the more spectacular forms have the traditional flower shape of radiating petals. In most, these petals have been greatly modified. Some, like the eucalypts, have assigned a protective function to originally delicate petals — they now form the operculum, capping the colourful stamens, and are shed when the flowers open. Others, including the melaleucas, retain reduced petals, but in the expanded flower these are eclipsed by the greater, brighter stamen bundles.

The pollen-tipped stamens, bunched or radiating in brush fashion, are often the showy, colourful part of Australian flowers. Others like *Dryandra* and *Banksia* have stiff, wire-like floral

Slender leaves of the Spreading Cone Bush, Isopogon divergens, *allow the pink flowers to show clearly though they are carried among foliage. In* Isopogon, *a cone develops beneath each flower head, and is later shed to release the seeds.*

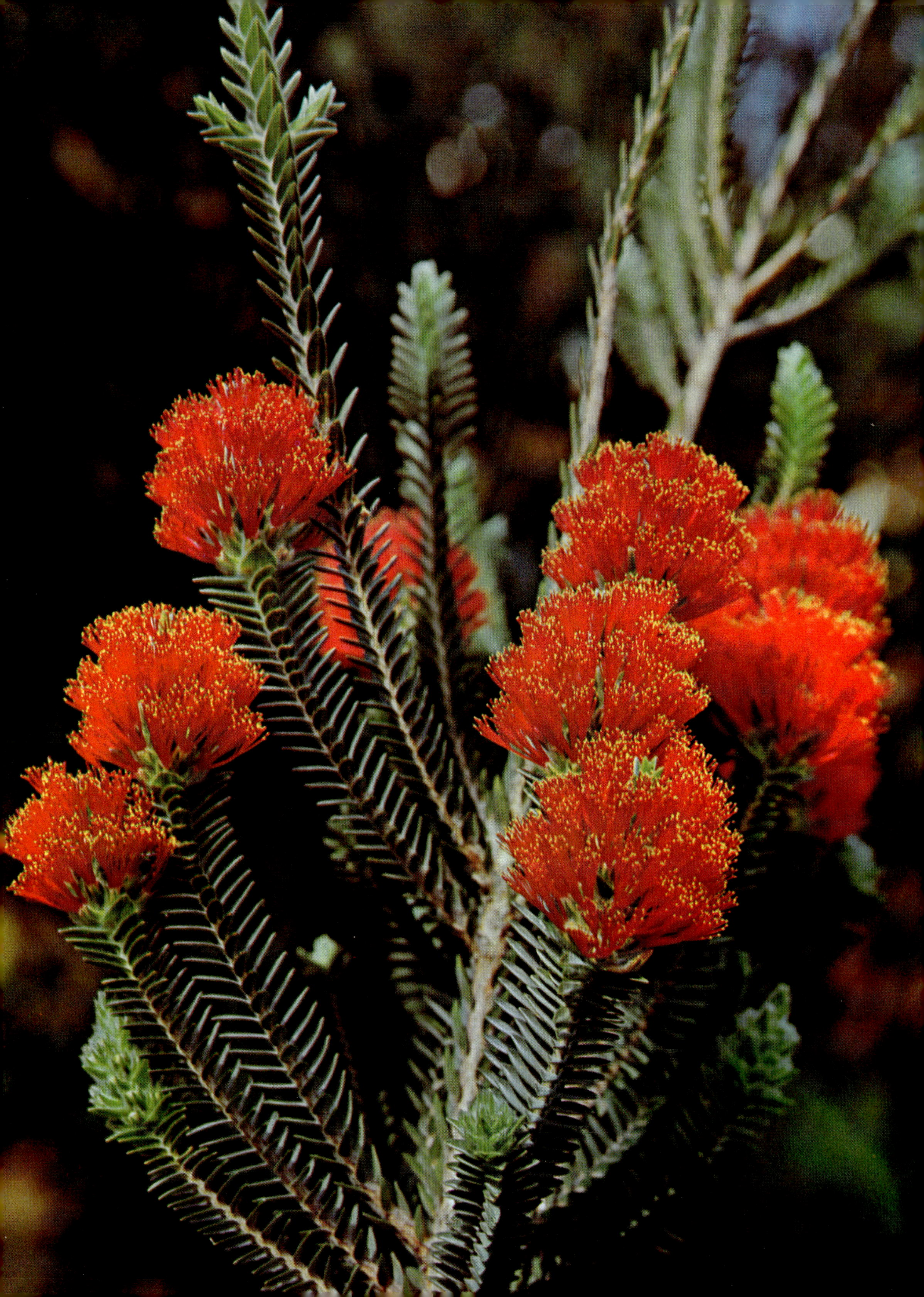

The Carnarvon Bird Flower, Crotalaria cunninghamii, *bears long racemes of green flowers which in shape resemble flying birds. It is also a bird flower in function, being pollinated by the avian honeyeaters. The petals, which form a keel beneath the flower, are rolled in a cone-like shape with a small opening at the apex through which pollen is forced. Through the same orifice emerges later the receptive stigma, so that a honeyeater having brushed against pollen at one flower would touch its pollen-dusted plumage to the stigma of a second flower.*

OPPOSITE:

A tall shrub reaching to twenty feet, the scarlet Regelia grandiflora, *is an outstanding western wildflower, but growing in south coast regions difficult of access it is not as well known as others less spectacular.*

These western sandplain ridges are alight with flame colours of the Sand Heath Bottlebrush, Beaufortia squarrosa. *These plains harbour many vivid wildflowers, but few so arresting as the crimson and orange expanses of* Beaufortia *in flower.*

structures, often with a burnished surface which resembles the sheen of a metallic finish, heightening the impression that each is an exquisite sculpture in metal rather than a living flower.

With other strangely shaped and coloured wildflowers including the kangaroo-paws; the multi-coloured, feathery-flowered verticordias; the rose-cone isopogons, and the pendant bells pimelias and darwinias which are not flowers, but their enclosing bracts brightly tinted and greatly enlarged, these flowering trees and shrubs and small plants are new and unusual to those accustomed to "conventional" or garden forms of flowers.

Though these wildflowers merit conservation for their strange beauty alone, they represent also the ages of evolution in an isolated corner of the world where primitive plants have persisted under conditions of aridity and sandy soil that have forced development of the most floriforous forms. In the company of the honeyeating birds which have long served as pollen carriers, many wildflowers have tended toward deep or tubular shapes, often, like the paws, unusual in the world of flowers but most efficient in the exploitation of avian honeyeaters.

Together with those that gain effect from foliage — the blue and silvered mallees and the stem-clasping, yellow, red and purple leaves of the Royal Hakea, *H. victoriae* — these wildflowers must be allowed a permanent place in the Australian environment. Each is unique: by the very nature of evolution, which can never exactly re-trace old paths, once lost not one of these wildflowers of Australia can ever be re-created.

Flowers of the Myrtaceae *are characterized by stamens as the colourful part of the inflorescence. These stamens are free and arranged in radiating, brush-like fashion on the flowers of eucalypts and callistemnons (bottle-brushes) but united in flat bundles in* Calothamnos sanguineus, *the Silky-leaved Bloodflower, and several others of the genus. The stamen bundles form a long tube, not unlike that of the kangaroo-paws, so that honeyeaters probing the deep flower must be daubed with pollen around forehead and cheeks by the anthers which form the "claws" of the paw.*

The Golden Paw, Anigosanthos pulcherrima, *flowers in summer months in company with other yellow-flowered sandplain wildflowers including golden species of* Verticordia *and* Banksia, *and the western Christmas Tree,* Nuytsia. *Both the branched stems and the flowers of rich yellow, sometimes suffused with red, carry a woolly surface and when not in flower the species can be recognized by this tomentum which extends also to the leaves.*

Flowering in September and October, White Clematis climbs rocks and shrubs of coastal forests, where it is then a prominent feature of the undergrowth. In the flowers of this Clematis pubescens, *petals are replaced as the conspicuous flower part by four, occasionally five, sepals. The seeds, before being scattered by the wind, are airborne in fluffy white masses, quite as attractive as the flowers.*

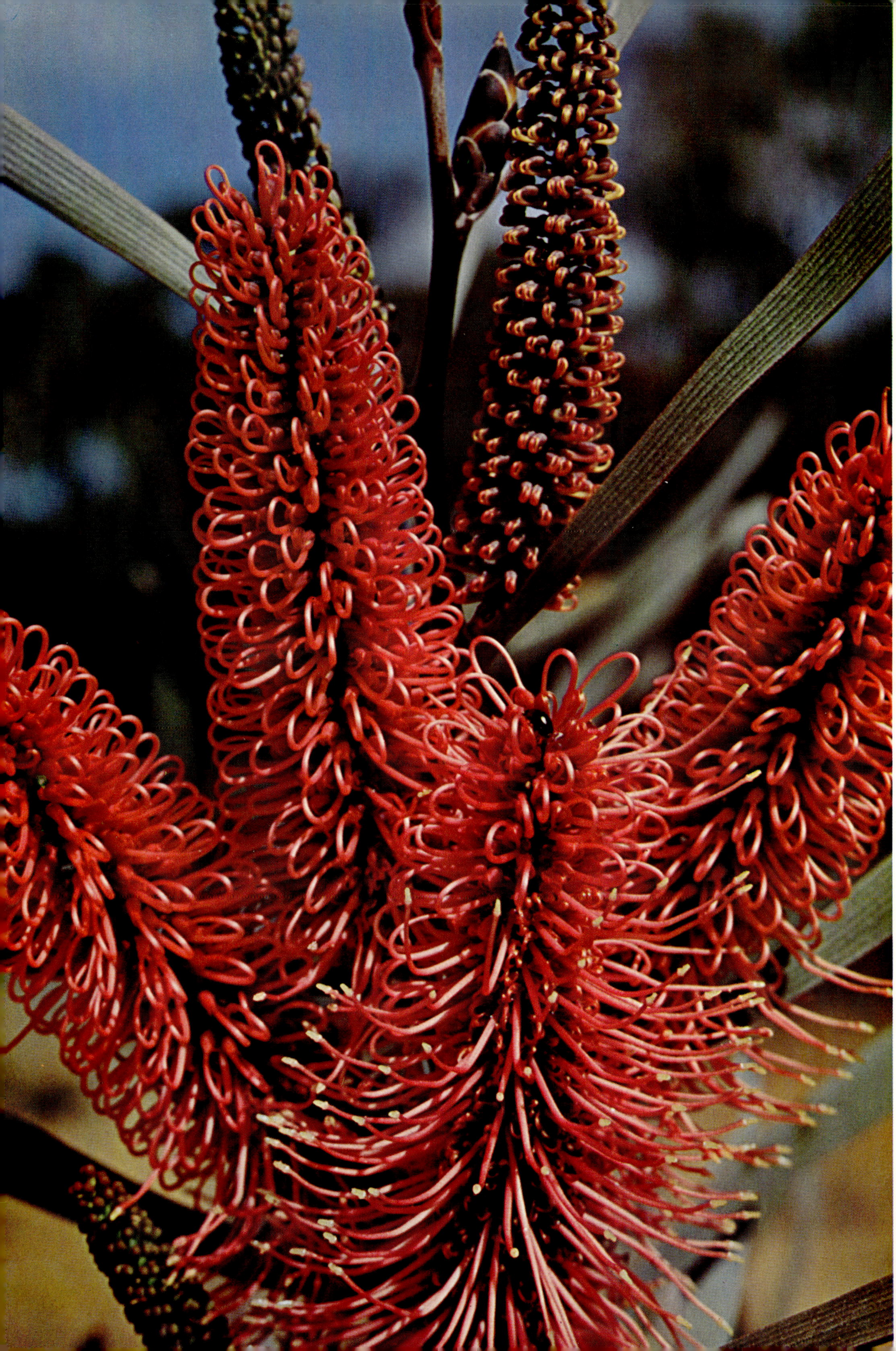

DEPENDENT ON WATER

SCATTERED SPARINGLY through a dry continent, lakes and swamps in Australia have become refuges for plant and animal life dependent on water. In the aquatic environment flora and fauna combine in compact communities supporting an exceptional variety and density of living things.

Though maps of Australia show great lakes often stretching in long chains through parts of the interior, most are dry salt lakes, some in the most arid parts being covered by a shallow sheet of water only on rare occasions, perhaps once in a decade. Most contain water for a month or two each year — if capricious rains reach inland. Like the permanent swamps, lakes and rivers of the moist coastal perimeter, these inland lakes have a wildlife population, with the life cycle of every creature geared to the nature of its temporary habitat.

Not surprisingly in a land where water is scarce at the best of times, and lakes more often dry than full, some creatures have moved from crowded watery habitats to occupy vacant niches in wider

A tall shrub exceeding twenty feet, and with six-inch flower spikes borne among narrow leaves on slender vertical stems or branches, Hakea multilineata *is one of Australia's hundred species of hakea. This form is common in western inland districts.*

Climbing a tiny ladder of stiff hairs, an ant moves towards the brink of a trap: the pitcher of the carnivorous plant Cephalotus follicularis. *Any insect that ventures near the brink will lose its grip on the waxy surface. Once in the digestive liquid it cannot escape, for the waxy walls are capped with an over-hanging lip and a palisade of downward-pointing spikes. It is thought that the carnivorous habit of this plant must supply nitrogen, deficient in the swampy soil. Pitchers are normally bright green, turning brick red with age and exposure to sunlight. Minute new pitchers, perfect in every detail, still have lids shut.*

Fungi are found universally wherever organic material is available and they require moist, warm conditions for their best development. Members of this great plant division have several characteristics in common apart from their lack of chlorophyll. They produce spores instead of seeds as a means of propagation; and though often colourful, possess neither flowers nor true roots. Their fine, branching filaments invade and destroy dead or living tissues, either plant or animal. Acting as scavengers, fungi bring about the breakdown of fallen trees and branches. Without them, debris would accumulate and choke the forest. Fine filaments web through every crack and pore of moist dead wood, bark or humus. When moisture, temperature and food supply are favourable, fungi of the Basidiomycetes group develop small "buttons" on the webbed mycelium, and in a sudden rush of growth break the surface to expand in mushroom shape. From delicate pores or gills beneath the cap the millions of microscopic spores may be blown far before settling, where, in damp conditions, each will crack and put out the first filament of a new mycelium web.

plains and bushland. Others threatened by the periodic drying of inland waterways have evolved the means to survive through long dry periods.

Australia's wildlife of coastal lake and swamp is for the most part less distinctive than its unique dry-land fauna. Foremost of the strange creatures of the continent are the furred animals, of which the waterways can claim only one of primitive distinction: the Platypus.

Among land birds, this continent has distinction in colourful parrots; in honeyeaters evolved for a land of wildflowers and mild climates; and in its true eccentrics — megapodes, lyrebirds, bowerbirds and emus.

Though the Black Swan, one of Australia's largest water birds, is an inevitable inclusion to any list of unusual members of the fauna, it is distinct only in colour, having as close relatives the swans of other continents. Shore birds and waders are cosmopolitan types: dotterels, sandpipers, pratincoles, oyster-catchers, gulls — most are summer visitors from other lands, or have closely related species around the world.

Among inhabitants of the reedbeds crakes, coots and swamp-hens are found abroad. Snow-white egrets, adorned with upswept, filamentous lacelike plumes in their breeding season, are, with herons and spoonbills, the most elegant of birds, but as nearly represent the avifauna of any other land as that of Australia.

Throughout the world the close similarity of water habitats has fostered a great likeness; of all birds, sea birds are the most cosmopolitan. Those seen on Australian beaches frequent the seashores around the globe. Almost as universal are the migratory waders and birds of the lake beaches, followed closely by herons, egrets and most other water-dependent birds. But in Australia permanent lakes and reedbeds are a feature only of the well-watered perimeter. In the interior, great extremes are encountered in saltlake and claypan habitats, demanding some degree of adaptation and specialization by most water-dependent creatures. Here some members of Australia's water community show distinction.

The birds, able to fly to other waters as lakes dry out, have adapted principally by breeding when and where conditions are optimal. Thus the rather rare Banded Stilt responds to the filling of inland lakes and the increasing abundance of the shrimps which constitute its principal food. The

Banded Stilt, *Cladorhynchus leucocephala,* occurs only in the interior of Australia, breeding in small colonies on the edges of salt lakes. From year to year these colonies shift to lakes where rain has provided optimum conditions of water level and salinity — factors governing the abundance of the brine shrimp. Consequently the nesting grounds of these stilts were not discovered until fourteen years after the naming of the bird.

In Australia where dry land is plentiful indeed, and water usually scarce, a number of water birds now fill dry-land niches perhaps previously unoccupied. Plovers and dotterels, principally birds of ocean, river and lake shores, have among their Australian species several which have forsaken the beaches to lead a bushland existence. The Australian Dotterel, *Peltohyas australis* has largely given up its waterside habits, nesting on the driest plains of the interior where the eggs are deposited in a shallow hollow on bare or stony ground, and may be covered with debris or pellets of hard earth when the bird leaves the nest to feed. Plovers also include former waders now exclusively ensconced in the dry-land habitat.

The Banded Plover, *Zonifer tricolor*, is most commonly encountered away from water, and often far from water on arid inland plains. It does not return to the waterside to nest, but deposits the eggs in a shallow scrape on paddocks or arid plains. In colour its three or four eggs vary from pale to dark olive-green, streaked and spotted with light to dark brown depending on the tones and texture of the soil of the nest environs.

Kingfishers are generally associated with fish hunting and a perch by lake or stream, but in Australia fishing by kingfishers is less common than bushland hunting. Most belong to the wood kingfisher group, *Daceloninae;* the true kingfishers (similar in appearance, but usually found patrolling streams, rivers or lakes and hunting by plummeting into the water from perched or hovering position) being represented in Australia by two *Alcedinidae* species only: the Little Kingfisher, *Alcyone pusilla*, and the Azure, *Alcyone azurea*. Wood kingfishers include not only the small, bright-plumaged birds but also the notorious Laughing Kookaburra, *Dacelo gigas*, and the more colourful north-western Blue-winged Kookaburra, whose laugh is more a fiendish cackle.

The small turquoise-plumaged Sacred Kingfisher shows a marked preference for nest hollows and hunting perches by the shores of swamps, where it preys on frogs and jilgies, but it is often found well away from any water, and may hunt for lizards, spiders and large insects. Most kingfishers are birds of tropical regions and of sedentary habits, but the Sacred, in a far-ranging migration, winters on islands of the latitude of Indonesia and nests in the southern summer along eastern and western coasts of Australia. The nest is a small hollow of a tree, often of a swamp paperbark, or occasionally is drilled into a termite nest. Here the young kingfishers are raised among incredible filth which accumulates as they grow, so that, like the underground-nesting bee-eaters, they hatch naked and develop feathers protected by enclosing waxy sheaths, which later split, to release plumage of the full azure and turquoise colours of the adult.

The favoured habitats of the White-fronted Chat include the samphire and saltbush margins of estuaries and inland waterways, where they nest on the low bushes.

Other species of this Australian family *Epthianuridae* are more colourful, bearing crimson, orange and yellow undersurfaces, but are

An alert Grey Teal watches from her nest. If alarmed, she would fly suddenly, leaving the eggs — a dozen or more — uncovered, but normally when leaving the nest, she pulls over a covering of down to conceal the eggs and retain their warmth.
This duck wanders over a great area: individuals banded in the Northern Territory have been recovered near southern coasts; others banded in the south west, have been shot in eastern states. The Grey Teal Anas gibberifrons, *is quick to nest after good rain at any time of the year, a characteristic enabling it to breed in normally arid inland regions.*

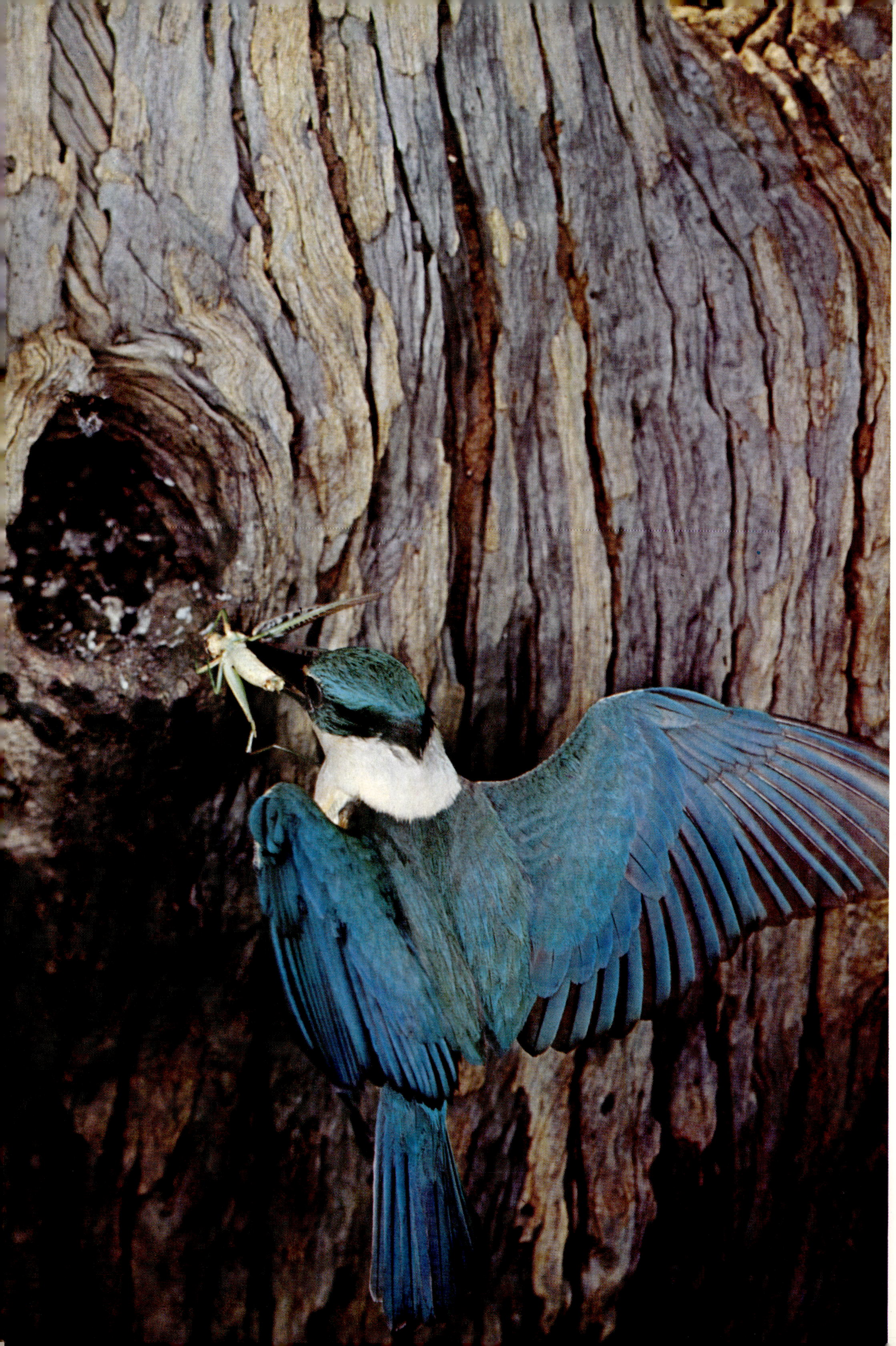

OPPOSITE:
An azure image against textured wood of a dead gum, a Sacred Kingfisher folds its wings to plummet into the knothole entrance of its nest.

In a continent of few rivers and streams, this kingfisher, **Halcyon sancta,** *preys normally on large insects, spiders, and on lizards. Sometimes showing a preference for swampland habitats, this bird then feeds on frogs and jilgies.*

Rising as a tall slender plant from moist spots along the south coast, this Swamp Bottlebrush, **Beaufortia sparsa,** *belongs to a genus of sixteen species, all confined to Western Australia.*

The Green and Golden Tree Frog, **Hyla moorei,** *is most often noticed on branches of paperbarks or other scrub of moist habitats. Brightly coloured green and gold in sunlight, this frog is capable of marked change to a dull brown pattern.*

A common spider of the reeds around swamps and marshes, the species **Argiope trifasciata** *wears silvered stripes over yellow and rust red tones, making it colourful and conspicuous on the web. Males are very much smaller, rarely seen except at the edge of the female's web.*

Building a miniature island for a nest, black swans are among Australia's best-known birds, their black plumage, a contrast to the chaste whiteness of swans in the northern hemisphere, helped perpetuate early stories of the southern continent as a land of differences. The Black Swan, Cygnus atratus, is quite abundant on coastal rivers, swamps and lakes. In flight, white wing tips, and at close range the red beak, bring added interest to uniform blackness of plumage.

birds of northern and far inland regions. Several show a preference for the samphire and saltbush flats; all nest after good rains at any time of the year.

Among the many Australian ducks must be mentioned the Musk, *Biziura lobata,* distinctive in behaviour and anatomy: both sexes have membranous lobes beneath the beak, but particularly large and conspicuous on the male, and prominent in his spectacular splashing, water-jetting displays. Musk Ducks normally fly only at night, otherwise taking refuge by rapid diving.

In the lake and swamp habitat, plants form the basis for life, often turning the water green with floating, microscopic phytoplankton, and in permanent swamps ringing the shores with reeds and bottlebrush scrub. Green plants are the food of countless insects and other small creatures, which in turn are taken by the larger hunters — but among swamp plants are some that turn the tables by preying on animal life. Soils bordering swamps tend to be deficient in plant foods, particularly in nitrogen which is easily leached away by seeping water. Perhaps it is to supplement a meagre supply of this element that the carnivorous *Cephalotus follicularis,* Albany Pitcher Plant, has devised leaves modified to form an effective trap and digesting organ.

This pitcher plant is restricted to swamp margins in a humid south-coastal crescent extending eastwards for perhaps a hundred and fifty miles from the extreme south-west corner of the continent, and represents an excellent example of parallel evolution, for similar pitchers of the genus *Nepenthes* are found on the rain-leached soils of mountain slopes in Malaysian jungles. Though similar in shape and function (*Nepenthes* pitchers are usually larger but have not the exquisite shape and colouration of the Australian form) the plants are not related: in each case the insect-trapping pitchers have evolved under similar conditions of moist habitat and deficient soil.

A second carnivorous plant endemic to the western coastal swamps is the Rainbow Plant, *Byblis gigantea,* a slender, upright shrub bearing deep-pink flowers, and with stems covered by glistening droplets on fine glandular hairs. The sticky secretions are able to hold and digest small insects. One insect, a small wingless capsid found only on these plants, is somehow able to traverse the viscid surfaces with impunity, feeding on the juices of flies caught on the traps of its sheltering host.

Though so many of the water birds are of cosmopolitan form, or but little distinguished from those of lakes and streams of other lands, the same could not be said of Australia's one distinctive furred animal of the watery habitat, the Platypus, which together with the spiny anteaters represents the order *Monotrema*, of ancient ancestry.

So different in appearance, habits and habitat, both platypus and anteater have the primitive egg-laying reproductive plan, and other slightly-reptilian characteristics. They have survived to the present only because they are highly specialized for exclusive niches: the platypus probably has been adapted for more than a million years to a life of underwater foraging in Australian lakes and rivers.

Some reptiles have shown extreme hardiness in adaptations to the desert environment; others have taken to rivers and marshes with equal ease. These water-dependent reptiles range from the huge salt and smaller freshwater crocodiles, water dragons and water skinks of the tropical north, to deadly tiger snakes of southern swamps.

More vitally dependent on water than any other land vertebrates are the frogs, which supplement lung breathing by oxygen transfer through skin that must be maintained in moist condition for survival. The vast majority are creatures of damp coastal regions where regular rains maintain the essential humid habitats, but some successfully inhabit semi-desert areas where heat and drought make conditions hostile for moist-skinned amphibians. These desert frogs too are dependent on water, but show some of the most outstanding developments for survival in quick breeding, deep burrowing, and water storing habits.

Though a paradox in form, the platypus is a mammal, primitive in some respects, but at the same time highly specialized. Early scientists failed to recognize the strange forms of duck-like bill and webbed feet as being adaptations to aquatic life; rather they were considered as degenerate or primitive features. The men of science were also uncertain of its mode of reproduction. It was almost a century after the discovery of the platypus that its egg-laying characteristic was finally confirmed. Mammals are of three classes, distinguished by reproductive development. Most primitive is the order Monotrema, *of which the Platypus,* Ornithorhynchus anatinus, *and the Spiny Anteater are the sole surviving members. Both lay soft-shelled eggs.*

The more advanced marsupials give birth to small, under-developed young, and more developed again in their manner of reproduction, are the placental mammals.

The "bill" of the Platypus is a soft leathery structure, extremely sensitive so that it can, with eyes closed, find all its food at the bottom of pool or river.

Burrows are constructed as a refuge: the elaborate breeding burrow may reach sixty feet in length, and terminates in a chamber where the female, behind earth barricades, remains curled around the two eggs until they hatch.

White-fronted Chats, dubbed "Tin Tack" for their call (a sharp metallic sound) are gregarious little birds of samphire and saltbush flats, and of shores, estuaries and lakes. The White-fronted Chat, Epthianura albifrons, *is found far into the interior, frequently in nomadic flocks, and has a wide distribution from southern Queensland to Tasmania and south-western Australia.*

A decorative grasshopper shows patterns and colours of its ventral surface. Long feelers mark it as a member of the long-horned family, Tettigoniidae. This individual is immature, and without wings. Unlike many insects, which undergo complete change from egg to larva, pupa and adult, the grasshoppers have an incomplete metamorphosis, hatching as small, wingless versions of grasshopper, but basically of adult shape. With successive moults, size and shape develop; the wings appear, and enlarge.

A Queensland Water Skink, Sphenomorphus quoyii, *unlike many of the Australian reptiles, enjoys a lush, humid habitat.*

The White-faced Heron, **Ardea novae-hollandiae,** *commonly frequenting swamps and the margins of lakes and streams, is found throughout Australia wherever there is suitable habitat. A bird of the shallow waters and mudflats, this heron takes frogs, jilgies, and various insects.*

Small green water plants mark the deep blue of a shallow swamp, and a solitary paperbark stands in the foreground. This is a favoured hunting ground of the wading birds — the herons, egrets, stilts, and dotterels. On the open water swim and feed the grebes and ducks. Distant scrub and reedbeds support a different fauna, and provide nesting sites for the waterfowl. In Australia most shallow swamps dry out between rains, so that creatures unable to fly to permanent water must, like the frogs and tortoises, hide encased in damp mud beneath the ground.

Red Kangaroos are inhabitants of the vast open grasslands and stony plains of the Australian outback.

FRONTISPIECE:

Warned by the light touchdown of the robin returning, downy grey young in a camouflaged nest rise up with orange mouths wide for the beakful of tiny insects he brings. To the widest gape will go the lot! An instant later the pink-and-grey female landed beside him at the nest. These Scarlet Robins, Petroica multicolor, are but one species of the many Australian flycatchers known as robins — among the others are Flame, Pink, and Rose-breasted Robins, a Hooded Robin, Yellow Robins, and White-breasted and Red-capped Robins.

FRONT COVER:

With sunset the bush animals appear from their hiding places in trees or burrows or nests of leaves and grass. In Australia most are marsupials: primitive forms now highly adapted in an isolated continent. This Brushtail Possum climbing towards upper branches and gumleaves is one of the most widespread of all Australia's creatures. It is found from the north down through N.S.W. and Victoria to South Australia, and in Tasmania, Western Australia and the Northern Territory.

BACK COVER:

Rust- and ochre-toned new growth shoots from buds at the base of the composite cone of a south-coast shrub, Banksia baxteri. The sandy southern and western coastal plains are the home of the best of Australia's magnificent genus Banksia.

PAGE SIX:

Pure stands of lofty Karri crowd Australia's southwestern corner, just surpassed in height by the Mountain Ash of the eastern coast. These gums rank among the world's highest, some topping three hundred feet.